"Alan is a type of unicorn in   has the most unique, yet bi much of Christianity is thwart predictable & limiting box, Ala.. ......  his personal experiences with this Jesus who is bigger than what New Age & Spiritualism can offer. I recommend that you get to know Alan and experience a brand new expectation of the Kingdom of God for yourself, business strategies and your leadership capabilities."

DANNY SILK
President of Loving on Purpose
Senior Team Leader of Bethel Redding CA

"I am so excited for Alan's new book *Spiritual Evolution*. As a deliverance minister, I have found Christian ignorance about the occult to be a major open door to the demonic realm. This book helps bring revelation to areas of disguised occult practices that have crept into the Church itself. Alan's personal experience in these practices will give you insight into truth."

DAWNA DE SILVA
Founder and Co-leader of Bethel Sozo
Bethel Transformation Center, Redding CA

"Congratulations, I loved the book, truly I did, I sensed such excitement in my heart as I read it and it carries FREEDOM, IT'S ANOINTED !!!

Thank you so much for sharing your journey with such honesty and Truth.

I believe there is powerful breakthrough into freedom from the deception that is in the New Age movement and is on the increase in this hour, not only for those who don't know Jesus but believers who are not anchored in the Truth, within the pages of your book.

The clear unfolding of your journey cuts through the confusion that has surrounded this subject for far too long. Yes again He has worked all things for good for you and for others who have the opportunity to read and share it.

It's a perfect size as well, and I can see it being placed in the hands of many souls that, as you are and have always been hungry for the Truth."

KIM JONES
Senior Leader, Liberty Family Church, Gosford, Australia
On the Board of Awakening Australia

"We are in a time of convergence where marketplace leaders and faith influencers are becoming one voice. Alan Strudwick is a voice that the Father has anointed to pioneer such a move. Thank you, Alan for communicating the heart of the Father to us and help point us in the direction that God is speaking!"

JAMIE GALLOWAY
Author of SECRETS OF THE SEER
Director of The Online Center for Dreams, & Prophetic Communicator.

SPIRITUAL EVOLUTION

[A NEW AGE LEADER'S
SHOCKING DISCOVERY OF TRUTH]

ALAN STRUDWICK

Copyright © 2020 by Alan Strudwick

All rights reserved. No part of this publication may be reproduced, distributed, or transmitted in any form or by any means, including photocopying, recording, or other electronic or mechanical methods, without the prior written permission of the publisher, except in the case of brief quotations embodied in critical reviews and certain other noncommercial uses permitted by copyright law. For permission requests, write to the publisher, at the address below.

Kingdom Business Publishing
www.kingdombusinessministries.com

All Scriptures used are from the New King James Version of the Bible unless otherwise stated

Printed in USA - Printopya

Library of congress Cataloging-in-Publication data
Strudwick, Alan. 1958 -
Spiritual Evolution : Life autobiography

ISBN 978-1-64570-590-1

1. Personal Development- Christianity. 2. Spiritual Development. 3. Christian Life Principles

First Edition 2020

Also available as an E-Book - Amazon – Kindle & Apple – ibook

[ACKNOWLEDGMENTS]

I would like to a thank my amazing wife Anne-Marie for her countless hours of editing…her insight and guidance over a 12 month period have brought this book to its completion. She worked on it when she felt like it, and when she didn't. We spent the last year travelling extensively and she faithfully carried the manuscript 'on the road' with her…constantly looking for another quiet moment to write.

Through her commitment to excellence, I believe this book has turned into a powerful, detailed and informative story of my life, my spiritual journey and my passion.

Thanks Babe!

[TABLE OF CONTENTS]

1. The Journey Begins — 1
2. My Invitation into Hinduism — 8
3. My Spiritual Advancement — 17
4. Trouble in Paradise — 26
5. A Shocking Encounter — 32
6. Truth Under The Microscope — 41
7. The Beginning of the End — 47
8. Out Of The Ashes — 55
9. True Enlightenment — 61
10. Mother Nature — 69
11. The Gift Of Truth — 82
12. When Evil Took Centre Stage — 94
13. Sleeping With The Enemy — 114
14. Yoga On Trial — 130
15. The Gods of Yoga — 148
16. The Asanas of Yoga — 154
17. The Way Home — 178

MY FAMILY ARRIVES ON AUSTRALIAN SOIL IN 1964

[THE JOURNEY BEGINS]

This is an account of one person's life, who embarked on a spiritual quest spanning 49 years. It was my journey - born from a heartfelt quest for love, peace and a deep hunger to encounter and experience higher realms of power.

In my early 20's I became a Leader in the New Age Movement. My spiritual journey will challenge some, yet I know, will bring freedom to others.

I have always been reluctant to tell my full story. Put simply – it's because it involves the detailed account of a deception so great that my life became entrapped for decades in an ongoing prison of lies. To be honest, I have never desired or been passionate about recounting my many dark encounters and experiences with evil principalities and powers that masquerade as 'angels of light'.

However, people have encouraged me to be bold and share the truth - to expose the deceptions and teachings of *false prophets* that are permeating the culture of our day, leaving so many confused and seeking for answers. I am all too aware that the *single greatest goal* of all deception is to lead people away from the truth, by firstly blinding their eyes. The next step is to wean them into a lifestyle controlled by a labyrinth of carefully crafted lies. Beyond this, and deception's ultimate goal, is to imprison lives by enslaving them into a system of endless and cruel religious practices and beliefs.

No human being deserves to live this life!

I have lived both sides. I stand as one who truly has verified life experiences of knowing the reality of both the dark and deceptive, as well as the light and truth.

As a former Leader in the New Age, my entire life's journey was focused on and consumed with *renouncing the deity of Jesus* and exposing the Christian myth that mankind could have a living relationship with a deeply personal God.

MY EARLY YEARS

My father's entrepreneurial dream was to relocate his Canadian born family to the new land of promise - Australia. This included my mother and siblings. Though his business life began to boom, his personal and family life told a different story. His marriage was soon over. My mother left, taking me and my siblings with her - she was desperate to start a new life for us all! She remarried sometime later.

Sadly, our household was traumatic. When I was 13, after several attempts to run away from home, the courts finally gave my father full custody. I moved into my father's household with his new wife, whose interest in spiritualism and Eastern religious practices matched his own. This became my new home environment.

A YOUNG HEART AWAKENED

I began my pursuit for spiritual enlightenment at the tender age of 11.

I grew up with two very strong influences over my life – both fostered by my father. The first was business. My father was a gifted entrepreneur whose business acumen continued to inspire me to follow in his footsteps. He bought me my first enterprise when I was 16 years old. He taught me all aspects of running a business, while I completed my last 2 senior years of high school. It was during this season of my life that I developed my passion for the business world.

The second strong influence came as a result of my father's deep hunger to explore *the world of the spirit*. His unbridled curiosity led him into an extensive search of the world of Eastern religions. This included the smorgasbord of New Age practices, the occult, and spiritualism.

I deeply loved my father and believed everything he told me.

He also had the available funds to create very real opportunities to shape my young life - both through the business world and the world of the spirit.

MY EARLIEST ENCOUNTER

At age 11, I remember being in the schoolyard with a group of boys. School yard adventures are usually relatively harmless, however, several of us had discovered a playground 'activity' that, in looking back, definitely wasn't all that safe. We would pick someone from the group to hyperventilate, and then stand behind them, squeezing their lungs until they would black out and fall to the ground! When it was my turn, I hyperventilated, then blacked out. While I was on the ground, I had a graphic 'vision' of my future - *I saw the man I was destined to become!*

I was between the ages of 40 to 50 years old and dressed in a business suit! I knew from that moment on, that my life would somehow be involved with the corporate world of business.

When I regained consciousness on the playground, I still felt like I was my *older self.* I remember thinking, '*Why am I back in my childhood?*' The experience was so real that it disorientated me for the next three days - I actually felt that I was from the future and had somehow returned to my childhood.

HUNGER FOR THE UNKNOWN

From that day on, I had a deep awareness that there was more to life than just me and my body, in the here-and-now - and then I die?! I knew there was a reality beyond this natural world. I sensed there was an unknown invisible world. And even as a young 11 year old boy, I knew my experience in the playground was inviting me to explore more deeply, the unchartered realms of the world of the spirit.

It was from this point onward that my youthful mind began to ask 'bigger' questions - *'Where do we go when we die?'* and *'Is there a way I can explore this other world while I'm still alive on this earth?'*

ALAN IN YEAR 6
I WAS 11 YEARS OLD WHEN I HAD MY FIRST "SPIRITUAL"
EXPERIENCE IN THE SCHOOL PLAYGROUND

2

[MY INVITATION INTO HINDUISM]

As I mentioned before, the woman my father married was heavily invested in Eastern religious practices, primarily the Hindu religion. My father's wealth meant he was able to fly highly officiated New Age leaders from India and parts of America, right into the comfort of our own home. Sitting at their feet as a young teen, I can remember my heart and mind hungrily leaning into everything they said. For hours, they would expound their teachings and instruction in Eastern religious practices to my newly converted parents.

It was our "boxed seating" to all things Hindu!

As I witnessed aspects of the supernatural flowing from these New Age leaders, it wasn't long before my inquisitive heart embraced the Eastern Hindu religion as my own.

A DEEPENING HINDU LIFESTYLE

As a consequence, my innocent yearning for spiritual experiences led me into a more serious pursuit of the supernatural. The gurus, who were more than happy to satiate the passion of a new devotee, began to teach and lead me through many new open doors of experience in the world of the spirit. As this new journey of discovery continued, I committed myself to learn everything that was made available to me.

My appetite for the supernatural became the driving force of my life. I dedicated as much time as I could to integrating every religious practice the gurus and teachers would put before me.

They provided me with an extensive 'smorgasbord' of spiritual experiences that I spellbindingly dived headlong into. Every new practice held the invitation to unlock another door into the mysteries of an unseen world. *A world I longed to access!*

Within a few short years, my steady progress into the realm of the spirit was noted by one of the Hindu gurus. I was invited into a sacred initiation under his singular leadership. This came with the promise of admission to higher levels of ascension. So, at the impressionable age of 13, I agreed to commence learning under my Guru's spiritual guidance.

I eagerly embraced the upgrade in his attention, believing that these were my first steps in discipleship training for the lifestyle of a true Hindu devotee.

IN PURSUIT OF NIRVANA

Under my Hindu Guru, I embraced many spiritual practices. Once a year I was taken through an initiation ritual to invoke a new Hindu god into my being. The purpose of 'yoking' with each new god, was to lead me into further realms of the spirit by chanting their specific names.

I was to perform my other spiritual exercises as well as chant the names of Hindu gods internally during the exercise of Eastern meditation. I was taught that the practice of internal meditation and chanting would clear *karma* in my lifetime here on earth, therefore setting me free from returning to earth again.

This was my path of enlightenment!

Under my Guru's instruction, the new goal set before my life was to grow strong enough spiritually so I could eventually transcend through the many spiritual realms that existed above the earth. I was promised that only then, I would be able to reach the ultimate quest of my life - *the god realm of Nirvana* or, becoming 'one' with the universe.

With this enticing promise of *full enlightenment* set before me, I remained wholly committed to a lifestyle in pursuit of deeper spiritual knowledge and practices. My spiritual voyage further fueled, by the ongoing 'reward' my Guru offered for my religious disciplines - *transcendence through each new level to a higher level of enlightenment.* Each year, my Guru would initiate me into the next level. He said I was a special soul, and I had been here on earth for over 300,000 lifetimes!

At last I had a 'grid' for what took place back in the schoolyard when I was 11 years old! I now believed my soul had *chosen* to come back to this lifetime, and seek higher learning in order to continue its evolvement to greater levels of enlightenment.

BASIC HINDU BELIEFS

Often within the mindsets of our Western culture, we find it difficult to embrace the ideologies and practices of the Hindu religion. As I delved into deeper layers of Hinduism, I discovered its mammoth complexities. It involves 100's of different gods, each identified by name, and requiring religious disciplines and practices of an equal number.

The most basic premise of Hindu philosophy, is that the human soul has many lifetimes allotted to it.

With this in mind, the Hindu religion believes that the soul needs to pass through a method of evolvement, by *clearing karma* and transcending through many lifetimes. This process of 'reincarnation' continues until the soul reaches the state of *Nirvana* - to become 'one' with the universe. This is touted as the final and most desired destination. *It is the place where each soul becomes an intrinsic part of the universe and the place of habitation for the Hindu gods: Braham, Vishnu, and Kali.*

The Hindu philosophy that is deeply embedded into their religious culture, is that if a soul has an intrinsic spiritual awareness in this lifetime, he or she has already begun moving toward *spiritual enlightenment* and the promise of accelerated evolvement to higher levels.

My own spiritual hunger had been recognized in my early years and resulted in my Guru initiating me into this process - he became my soul's spiritual guide.

THE KARMIC ORDER OF LIFE

The Hindu belief system is that our soul starts out as an inanimate object, such as a rock. It then progresses upwards through a specific order. It begins with plant life, followed by animals, and ending when the soul finally 'evolves' into human existence. The simple rule of *karma* is this – if you do good things in this lifetime you move ahead into higher realms of spiritual evolvement. Alternatively, if you do bad things in this life, your evolvement (or soul) moves in a backward direction.

It is the Hindu's core belief that living on earth is the training ground for evolvement. It is the place where karma is cleared.

AN UNCOMFORTABLE TRANSITION

There is one major instruction that was carefully omitted from Hinduism's entrance into Western culture - *the evolvement of women!* In its purest form in Eastern culture, the ancient Hindu scripts - the Upanishads, state that *"No woman can ever evolve to the godhead."*

Allegedly, a woman has an 'inferior soul' and is therefore regarded as having a lower spiritual life and thus, unable to transcend to a higher order of karmic life!

There is however, one exception to this Hindu tradition. If a woman chooses to serve man well in her lifetime, the god Braham may allow her to re-enter life as a man in her next lifetime on earth, and therefore continue her soul's evolvement.

The Upanishads state that only men can release karma!

Later, when we agreed as a movement to 'package' Hindu practices into Western culture, we knew that we had no chance of being received well if the role of women were to be diminished or minimized in any way.

We therefore chose to carefully and strategically omit this particular Hindu belief and practice from our teachings.

Another 'undigestible' practice followed under a Hindu belief system, is that people who are begging on the streets aren't offered the support we would give in Western culture. The Hindus believe that these individuals are suffering in this lifetime as a result of doing something *bad* in their last lifetime. So to help these people, would interfere with their spiritual journey of *clearing karma*, and therefore hinder their evolvement into a higher realm in their next lifetime.

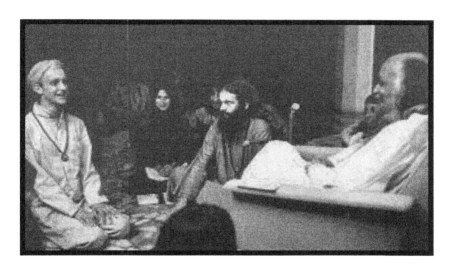

A WESTERN "DEVOTEE" RECEIVING RELIGIOUS
INSTRUCTION
FROM A HINDU GURU

[MY SPIRITUAL ADVANCEMENT]

For many of my teenage years and into my early 20's, I sat under my Guru's singular instruction. I advanced quickly through different levels of spiritual practices, as he continued to initiate me into higher planes of ascension. My Guru believed that my advancement was so significant in the realm of the spirit, he suggested that in the future, I could possibly have the privilege of living and traveling with him - and become a part of his elite 'inner circle' of devotees.

I was 100% committed and dedicated to this spiritual course as my life's full focus!

As an outworking of this focus, I further trained in every spiritual practice that existed. Below is a list of the practices I trained in and completed:

- Hatha Yoga
- Polarity Balancing
- Aura Cleansing
- Astral travel
- Soul Travel
- Rebirthing
- Meditation - all forms of eastern, Hindu and TM (Transcendental Meditation)
- Physic readings
- Tarot Reading
- Palm reading
- Soul transcendence
- Spirit Guide Visitations
- Physical Healing by transference
- NLP (Neuro Linguistic Programming)
- Alpha Dynamics
- Silva Mind Dynamics
- Mind Reading
- Mind Manipulation
- Prana Breathing Practices
- Hypnosis
- Super Learning
- Personal Development Seminars
- Soul Counselling
- Transactional Analysis
- Levitation

- Sound Current Energies
- Chakra Healing and Balancing
- Ying Yang Energy Balancing
- Past life Therapy
- Rebirthing
- Channeling,
- Spiritual Medium (contacting the dead)
- Clairvoyance
- Transpersonal Psychology
- Divination
- Chi and Ki force
- Reiki

At the end of my years of training, I became a fully functioning practitioner, teacher and spiritual guide in most of the above practices. I also achieved Master status in several of them, including Hatha Yoga.

THE REALIZATION OF MY DREAM

At the age of 22, I was accepted into the US Training Program to become a facilitator of the Personal and Professional Development arm of the organization my Guru had founded.

The bias of the Program was to launch a major integration of Eastern religious beliefs into Western culture, using the vehicle of Personal and Professional Development Seminars.

Through this Training Program, I now had the opportunity to give full expression to all my years of intensive training in spiritual practices.

We ran a five day Intensive Personal and Professional Development Seminar every month throughout the USA, Europe and Asia, with enrolments numbering from 100-250 people. We offered Advanced Development Seminars and also ran week long spiritual retreats.

During these training session 'cycles', I found my life's passion being realized - to teach and train others what I had learnt.

This passion was duly noted by the organization, and I was promoted to *lead facilitator* in the advanced seminars. This opened doors to new levels of influence on the USA speaker's circuit.

Many of the speakers who were household names, and the gurus of the personal development world, became my friends.

Our organization now had accredited open doors of influence to bring our spiritual beliefs and practices into mainstream Western society.

OUR TARGET MARKET: THE WORLD OF BUSINESS

My Guru believed if we could successfully market Hinduism in a palatable form into Western culture, we could gain a substantial increase in the religion's credibility. He also believed the 'vehicle' that would provide the greatest *target market* for our infiltration, was the business world. My Guru had founded a consulting firm, for which I interned, and then became an active consultant.

I was the perfect candidate to infiltrate the business world. My father had instilled his entrepreneurial acumen into me from an early age.

This target market strategy was outworked through the consulting arm of our organization, together with the trainings we offered through our ongoing seminars.

Our plan was to consult to high level management tiers of major business organizations with a singular focus: *to gain influence to leverage our Hindu beliefs and New Age practices into Western culture.*

I was amazed at how readily people accepted our teachings, as we carefully delivered our marketing plans and presentations to them. During my extensive seminars, I witnessed many well known businessmen and women, as well as celebrities who willingly embraced our Eastern practices as they sat fully attentive in our seminar conference rooms.

OUR PLAN: INFILTRATE AND DOMINATE WESTERN CULTURE

Because of the recognized gift I had to teach and train, I was also soon invited to become a leader responsible for mentoring new facilitators into the organization. This promotion also led to invitations into more 'secret' meetings ran by the organization.

These were restricted to the 'inner circle' of leaders and gurus of the New Age Movement world wide.

BEHIND CLOSED DOORS

Our primary focus for discussion in these meetings, was to strategize and target the spread of Eastern and New Age beliefs and practices into the Western world. Thirty years ago we were only too well aware that our Eastern beliefs and practices were generally unacceptable to the mindset of the average Westerner. We knew we were often seen and labelled as 'weird' and our practices 'unorthodox' and definitely *not* a palatable fit with the mainstream culture of the day.

This critical awareness meant that every discussion revolved around our plans to infiltrate and dominate Western Society.

Overall, we believed that it was possible to change an entire culture within a 30 year period!

We also recognized that another powerful 'weapon' of infiltration into the heart and foundation of societal culture, was through the acquisition of prominent and community focused industries. With this in mind, our organization developed a university, created health and medical centers, and purchased hotels and business consulting firms.

Today, many would be surprised at the number of 'community focused' industries that are owned by New Age or Hindu based organizations.

FOCUS ON CHRISTIANITY

Another focus group we planned to target and infiltrate, were *Christians*! We saw them as the least evolved on the planet – being here for their very first lifetime! Our strategic plan was to 'water down' Christianity as a faith and replace it with New Age philosophies and practices.

Over the years of my uncompromised involvement as a New Age Leader, I was personally responsible for leading many Christians away from their belief in Jesus as the Son of God, to a 'Hindu Jesus' who was a spiritual avatar, prophet or universal Christ -we called it 'Christ consciousness'!

Today, as an observer of our current spiritual culture and the many Eastern practices that are now the accepted 'norm', even by Christians, I would have to say that, our goal of changing the spiritual culture of the West, within a 30 year period, has actually succeeded!

ALAN FACILITATING A NEW AGE PERSONAL AND
PROFESSIONAL DEVELOPMENT SEMINAR - 1986

[TROUBLE IN PARADISE]

So here I was in my late 20's and living the life I had always dreamt of - I was travelling extensively throughout the US, Asia and Australia, and sharing the speaking circuit with men more than double my age. My title of Lead Facilitator gave me the privilege of speaking to countless hundreds of people in our Professional and Personal Development Seminars in each city. My life's purpose was being realized before my eyes – to invite and train countless others to follow my personal path of enlightenment, offering them the same mystic wisdom, philosophies and Eastern practices that I had passionately embraced from my own Guru's life and teaching.

The number of our seminars, spiritual retreats and teachings had begun to increase, moving from the tens to the hundreds, within the organization's world wide network. Our influence was indeed on the rise and this growth was exciting for me on a personal level – my heart's passion was to know that my life was making a difference in other people's lives.

I was 'living the dream'...or so I thought.

CLOUDS ON THE HORIZON

Running congruently alongside our success and based on the feedback from some of our course attendees, some stranger and more disturbing results were beginning to surface and be brought to my attention.

Regularly, and more consistently than I wanted to believe, we were receiving notification of strange results occurring in the lives of some of our course participants. This ranged from:

- Family members contacting us concerned about the strange behavior of a participant on their return from our courses.
- People having diagnosed psychotic episodes and being taken into psychiatric care.
- People were walking out on their marriages and their children.
- People were leaving their jobs.
- We were informed that people were even taking their own lives after the course. One of the most tragic incidents was a man I knew personally, who set fire to himself in his driveway in front of his wife – tragic!

I was unable to bury or push aside the deep and heartfelt concern I had for those who had innocently joined our courses, in the hope of improving their life's journey – only to end up with devastating and traumatic results in their own lives. This was *not* ok for me – not as a facilitator of our courses, nor as a human being wanting to bring peaceful and 'spiritually enlightened' solutions to the hearts of men and women within our sphere of influence.

Outwardly, I continued to live successfully on my life's 'stage', fulfilling all of my religious practices and duties, and running our many seminars across the world. However, a nagging and constant ache in my internal world told me things weren't as they had been. I soon came to recognize that it was the voice of my own heart's discontent. It came as an empty echo from somewhere deep within – a silent scream wanting attention and begging for answers. *And it simply refused to be silent any longer!*

BRAVE CONFRONTATION

During this lengthened season of unsettledness, I decided to approach my Guru, desperately hoping that his clarity and spiritual enlightenment would bring answers to my burdened and disquieted heart. I knew this was a somewhat risky move as we had been taught by the organization that any committed and enlightened devotee who began doubting 'the way' by asking too many questions, could be showing signs of regressing backward in their levels of enlightenment. This was seen as a serious issue, both to the gurus and to the devotees. I did not want to wear this label from my Guru, however, my desperate need for answers at this point was greater than my fear.

As I bravely opened my questioning heart to my Guru, I was unprepared for his cut and dried answer. He simply said, *"Some people on the planet are not evolved enough to handle the energy and spiritual practices we are creating."*

I had been taught over and over from the very beginning of my training sessions with my Guru, that there was no such thing as evil.

My heart deeply unsettled, I pondered, *'Then what other name could I give to these shocking events if they were not called evil?'*

I left his presence disquieted, feeling that I now had more questions than I had started with.

SEMINAR ATTENDEES RECEIVING INSTRUCTION FOUNDED ON OUR NEW AGE PRACTICES AND HINDU PRINCIPLES

5

[A SHOCKING ENCOUNTER]

As my heart continued on its own course, a *defining moment* helped me understand the 'language' it was trying to speak to me.

During one of the Personal Development Seminars I was facilitating, I decided to complete the student's pre-questionnaire form, rationalizing that it would help me become more *intuitive* on how I taught.

One of the questions on the form was:
>Q: *If you could have anything you want and without any limits, what would that be?*

My answer was:
>A: *I want a more personal connection to my godhead and the universal spirit.*

A DEFINING MOMENT

As a part of my facilitation process during the course of the seminar, I was to lead the participants through a guided imagery exercise. On this particular day, as every other time, I began to invite the participants into deeper states of imagery. I was practiced at the process, and familiar with the usual insightful outcomes that people experienced as they followed my lead.

What I wasn't prepared for – was what happened to me during this particular exercise!

I saw myself being taken into, what looked like, an underground cave. As I entered the cave it became intensely bright. As I adjusted my eyes, I saw a prominent and all powerful 'being', whom I believed to be God. There was a brilliant light surrounding him! I then noticed a *man* sitting on his right-hand side. *I'm not sure how, but I instinctively knew it was Jesus!*

At that time, I had never read a bible, and my only acknowledgement of Jesus, was what I had been taught by my Guru - that he was a man, or at best a prophet, and nothing more.

As I stood there, transfixed before him, Jesus told me to extend my hands out in front of me. And as I did, *beams* saturated with intense liquid light emanated from his hands and came into mine. He explained it was for me to use - to bring healing to others!

To say I was impacted by this experience would be an understatement! Strangely, I was now left with the feeling that this unorthodox vision might have something to do with the unsettling journey my heart was taking me on.

STRANGER STILL

On the last day of that seminar, I felt an unusual and very strange desire to visit a church.

The Cambridge Dictionary defines the word *strange* as the following:

> Unusual, unexpected, difficult to understand, to feel uncomfortable, not normal not known or familiar.

The above definition described *exactly* how I was feeling, yet no matter how many times I tried to rationalize the urge away, it simply wouldn't leave me.

To further explain my predicament, and how 'out of character' it was for me, it will help you to know that I had been completely indoctrinated by my Guru. He had taught me that Christians were on this planet for their very *first* lifetime, and therefore the least 'evolved' people group on the face of the earth. He told me that I, however, had been here for 300,000 lifetimes (this religious dogma deliberately targets the ego of man).

So therefore, knowing this, you can appreciate my dilemma. I was faced with the frustratingly annoying question, *'Why then would I want to go to a place and be surrounded with people who were not 'evolved' and ignorant to my true path of enlightenment?'*

The only somewhat rational thought that I was able to come up with was, *'Perhaps the universe is going to open up a portal of opportunity for me to step onto the stage of the church and instruct the ignorant Christians into the 'true' way of enlightenment?'*

This singular thought excited me - I was elated to think that the spirit world, together with the universe, had chosen me for such a key purpose – to help Christians evolve spiritually. Remember that one of the deepest desires of my heart, though misguided, was to help people on their life's journey towards spiritual enlightenment.

I asked my mother, who had been living in her area for many years, if she knew of any church in her neighborhood that I could go to. She gave me the address of a church that met in an industrial warehouse. As I neared the building, I heard what I thought was music for an aerobic class. I was curious. This did not fit any grid in my mind for 'church'! I walked past the door and saw what looked like a couple of hundred people singing and worshipping their Christian God - some with their hands raised upward.

As I stepped inside the building, I was directed by an usher, to sit in the third row from the front – I thought, *'A perfect position for me to make my move towards the stage when the universe directed me!'*

I waited and waited. Nothing happened.

Or did it?

As I sat patiently waiting, I was listening to the preacher on the platform. He used the phrase: *"Jesus as Lord of our lives"* and used the word *yoke* to describe our 'initiation' into this journey with Jesus. This spiked my attention as I knew all about 'lords' and what it meant to *yoke* them into my life. Yoking is also a term used in the Hindu religious culture, and one that I was very familiar with. It describes the process of initiation when you choose to join (or yoke) yourself to Hindu gods.

AN EASY YOKE

The preacher continued to hold my attention by his description of what type of 'lord' this Jesus was. He highlighted passages from the book of Matthew to explain what he was like:

> *"Come to Me, all you who labor and are heavy laden, and I will give you rest. Take My yoke upon you and learn from Me, for I am gentle and lowly in heart, and you will find rest for your souls. For My yoke is easy and My burden is light."*
>
> MATTHEW 11:29,30 NKJV

As the preacher spoke, my heart began to burn, *'Was it possible that there was yet another 'lord' that I hadn't yet met? A lord who described himself as being gentle? Who promised rest for my heavy and weary soul? Was there in fact an actual 'lord' that existed who claimed his "yoke was easy, and his burden was light"?*

I knew all the Hindu lords I had yoked with had enslaved my life to theirs. They became my masters, bringing a stream of difficult problems into my life so I could clear karma and evolve.

This was not what I was hearing about this new Lord, Jesus!.

When the preacher ended his talk, he asked if anyone would like to step forward and invite Jesus into his or her life as Lord. I thought, *'Why not?'* To me this process was the same as what I was used to when I invited Hindu lords into my life during initiations with my Guru. So I reasoned that I was simply asking Jesus into my life as another 'lord'.

AN ENCOUNTER WITH POWER

I stepped to the front and followed the preacher's prayer to ask Jesus into my heart. What happened next - I had no 'grid' for!

A singular wave of power hit my spirit like a bolt of lightening and more intense than anything I had ever felt before! Over my long history in the New Age, I knew what spiritual power felt like, but this encounter with power was different! (It was only sometime later that I was able to reference what happened to me, as the experience of being 'born again' through the power of the Holy Spirit).

Following this experience, the group who had responded to the preacher's invitation, were ushered into another room. Here, it was the task for designated team members from the church, to bring clarity and offer prayer to their new Christian converts.

The young man who had been assigned to speak with me, got more than he bargained for that day! When he told me I had just become a Christian, I vehemently and unapologetically informed him, *"NO, I AM NOT!!"*

He, though somewhat surprised, gently responded with, *"Yes, you are!!"*

I assured him by saying, *"NO! I just asked Jesus to come into my spirit, along with all the other lords I already have!"*

The more the poor guy tried to explain, the angrier I got, until finally my anger got the better of me – I swore in his face and abruptly left the room.

QUESTIONS, QUESTIONS, QUESTIONS!

In the days ahead, as I processed my somewhat confused and questioning heart, I had to admit that something supernatural and unexplainable had happened to me that day. However, I still could not, in any way, reconcile with the young man's dogmatic statement, that I *"had become a Christian!"*

With almost two decades of Hindu indoctrination in place, I could not accept that this one incident had erased the entire foundation and core of my religious beliefs and structure.

And nor would I!

PASTOR PHIL PRINGLE - HEAD PASTOR OF CHRISTIAN CITY CHURCH, BROOKVALE

IT WAS THIS MAN'S MESSAGE THAT INSPIRED ME TO TAKE THE BOLD STEP TO INVITE JESUS INTO MY LIFE IN NOVEMBER 1987.

A Shocking Encounter

[TRUTH UNDER THE MICROSCOPE]

Though the reality of my own mind assured me that I *definitely hadn't become a Christian*, I did have to acknowledge that *something* had actually happened to me! This left me with more questions about this new 'lord' Jesus, than answers.

I have always considered myself a 'healthy' skeptic, and one who has never been willing to simply accept someone else's truth as my own. My attitude throughout life has been to thoroughly research and investigate an issue in question, before I either agreed or disagreed with it.

Of course, this meant that the *only* course forward for me when it came to this new 'lord', was to thoroughly investigate him, until my heart knew the certainty of truth.

MY PILGRIMAGE BEGINS

As I began my journey of discovery, the first thing I did, was to buy myself a Bible. I obviously had never read one, as I had only been exposed to the ancient Hindu teachings of my Guru. As I looked at the massive volume of writings before me, my heart remained unwavering. I was determined to find out everything written about this one called Jesus.

Remaining true to my skeptical nature, my decision was to test him out as a 'lord' over the next 12 months. I told no-one in my world what I was doing. I continued with all my New Age practices - this included my meditations, along with two hours of spiritual exercises per day, including my chanting rituals. I continued to run seminars and meetings for the organization and remained committed to a once a month intensive study discourse from my Guru.

For all intents and purposes, my life looked exactly as it had before.

JESUS ON TRIAL

My 'test' to prove or disprove the authenticity of Jesus, was easy. I simply decided that *everything* that was written in the scriptures that he instructed me to do, I would do! For example, if I had sickness in my body, and I read that *Jesus healed sickness*, then I would search the Bible until I found out *how* he healed, and then I would simply and naively apply this truth to my life.

Over and over, as I followed his instructions through the [scrip]tures, I experienced results that could *only be called super miracles!*

To do with the area of healing, I remember one particular incident that perfectly describes this.

During my teenage years, when I would engage in certain physical activities, it was common for me to 'throw my back out' - this meant that any bending movement was not only restricted, but accompanied with excruciating pain. Whenever this happened, I was fortunate enough to be able to go to my Dad, who was also a practicing chiropractor. He had discovered from x-rays, that the problem with my back was the result of my right leg being shorter than my left. So any time I was in pain, he would solve the problem by giving me a chiropractic manipulation. After my Dad died, I no longer had access to this easy 'fix' for my back.

I remember once during my 12 month test of Jesus, I threw my back out. Once more, I decided to search the Bible to find out what Jesus said to do. I saw instructions that talked about *"laying hands"* on any area of sickness and using *"the name of Jesus"* to be healed. I decided to simply try it. I stood up, laid hands on my back, and told it, *"To be healed in the name of Jesus!"*

I was not expecting what happened next! I heard a series of loud 'cracks' and my back involuntarily clicked back into place!! I was so startled by the noise of bones being *manipulated into place*, I spun around, to see who was behind me! There was no-one behind me! I stood there, stunned by what had just happened - *my body was now free of all pain!* My heart was elated - I had no-one else to accredit this healing miracle to, except this 'lord' Jesus! *(As a side note, from that day until now, I have never needed another chiropractic manipulation for any back pain!)*

I began to see other miracles happen in my life, and it seemed to me, that *whatever* I had need of, this Lord Jesus, was not only able to fix it for me, but he was showing me again and again, that *he wanted to!*

This also included my financial needs - I would simply find out what Jesus said to do. I would then follow his teachings, and watch miraculous results unfold.

This truly was an amazing journey of discovery for me!

When I felt emotionally taxed - either anxious, sad, stressed or depressed, I would read incredible promises from the heart of Jesus, offering me his peace in the midst of every emotional storm that my life was facing. My heart was stilled in *every single instance*, as I eagerly embraced all that he offered me.

On this journey, there was something else that was radically impacting my heart. It was the discovery that this Jesus also revealed himself as a *God of love*. This was brand new 'language' for my heart - a God who loved? Surely this had to be the true *Nirvana* that every heart of man hunger's for?

My list of positive encounters with this new lord Jesus, kept growing as the weeks of his 'trial' slipped into months. I had begun to admit that *His yokes* were in every way, easier than the Hindu lords I had yoked to - they only ever brought pain, suffering and sadness to my life - all in the name of 'spiritual evolvement'.

I also had to admit the *only burdens* that this Jesus offered me, were in all truth, *lighter* than any I had ever experienced before. This also included a rare phenomenon for me – *the experience of joy!!*

I remember once, during this 12 month 'trial' period, I was in an ashram (a spiritual hermitage or monastery), and instead of chanting the names of Hindu lords internally, which I was always required to do, I decided to chant the name *"Jesus"*! As I began chanting his name, I felt a deep peace envelop my heart, and flow into every part of me. It was a peace beyond anything I had ever known. In fact, it took me by surprise and was so all encompassing, that I broke out in uncontrollable laughter. *Pure joy began to well up in me!* I felt it 'bubble' up from somewhere deep within me, as if someone had unplugged a well that refused to be contained any longer.

I remember that day only too well – my uncontrollable joy was bringing too much disturbance to the other devotees in the ashram, and I was 'not too politely' asked to leave!

It was sometime later that I learnt my experience in the ashram, was the contagious joy that the Holy Spirit releases into the life of a believer!

7

[THE BEGINNING OF THE END]

Twelve months earlier, the 'healthy' skeptic in me had made a decision to explore Jesus as a 'lord' – until I knew the truth.

And now, twelve months later, my skeptical heart was settled. The only conclusion I was able to come to, was the fact that Jesus as a 'lord', *was far superior in every way to all my other Hindu lords and gods!* I reached this conclusion, not based purely on factual knowledge, but the undeniable truth of my life's experiences with him during that period of time.

At last my heart was able to stop asking questions!

With my new focus now on Jesus as a superior Lord, I continued to facilitate our New Age Professional and Personal Development

Seminars, spiritual retreats, and advanced courses of enlightenment, however, now I was enthusiastic to reveal a God who surpassed all others!

At each of my events, I began to talk to our participants about my 'new' journey and my experiences with Jesus. I watched sadly, as time and again, many would quietly and deliberately get up and leave the room. A similar thing began to happen when I shared with my friends – instead of willingly embracing my new revelation of truth, they expressed their concerns saying that I *"was strange!"*.

RUN FOREST! RUN!

Undaunted by the seemingly 'cool' reception I was receiving from others, I decided that at the very least, my Guru would understand. After all, he was the one who had taught me everything I knew about evolvement on the journey to enlightenment. *He had also declared that all paths lead to God..*

I was now ready and enthusiastic to reveal a God who surpassed the ones he gave me, and that, *miraculously,* I had found a better path to God! This Lord Jesus was offering his followers the promise of going *straight to heaven when they died*, and his only 'ask' was that they simply accepted him as their Lord and Savior. This meant that *no-one* had to 'evolve' through thousands of lifetimes of suffering here on earth. They were immediately able to enter into heaven at the end of their lives.

'Surely', I thought, my Guru, would be positively affected by the impact of this great news...

I couldn't have been more wrong!!

What happened next, my mind still feels incapable of processing. As I sat before my Guru and began sharing my revelation of Jesus, his face began to contort. At the same time, the anger in his voice began to escalate, as he 'spat' out words of *"denial!!"* I watched, incredulous, as the man I had known for the past 20 years, changed before my eyes. A cloak of darkness settled over him, and for the first time I saw evil personified. *I was scared and he was furious!*

He stood to his feet and screamed at me, *"GET OUT!"*

This experience unsettled me for days. I even remember sitting on a plane heading from LA to Australia some time later, and still feeling the disturbing effects of that meeting.

When I arrived on Australian soil, I was greeted with the news that my Guru had *thrown me out of the movement!* He had faxed a worldwide communication to every organization we were involved with, stating the following:

- *Alan has contracted the 'red monk disease'* (I didn't even know what that was!)
- *Alan has lost his spiritual path*
- *Stay away from Alan, or he will contaminate you*

DAMAGE ASSESSMENT

As the full impact of this news hit me, I reeled in total shock. This one strategic piece of communication literally marked the end of my entire world. Everything that had been a part of my life was now taken away. Every purpose, every goal, every dream, every achievement - all gone in a matter of days! I was stripped of every title I had ever been given, and every project I was involved in for the organization was taken from me.

I was devastated!

Everything - this included every financial commitment that the organization had made to my life, *was now gone* - including the apartment that I lived in. The only single thing that was left in my world, was my BMW. This was owned outright by me. After living my entire life for the New Age organization, they had turned on me. Now my BMW, the only reminder of my past life, was parked outside a borrowed pup tent in a camping ground – now, my new 'home'!

As I desperately tried to put the pieces of my life back together, I continued to ask myself, *'How could free-spirited and spiritually 'evolved' people treat me this way, when all I was guilty of, was discovering a 'better' path? After all, wasn't this what we were all seeking for?'*

COLLATERAL DAMAGE

I think one of the saddest 'fallouts' for me personally during this time, was facing the fact, that the organization who had been my 'family' for so many years of my life, now saw me as an *outcast*, and called me "*unclean*". No-one would see me or even talk to me. This included even the closest of my friends. People who I had served with and helped - people who looked up to me – every single one abandoned me. It took 5 years before my best friend would even talk to me and when we finally did catch up for coffee, we had to meet in a 'hidden' location… *for his protection!*

Thankfully, my father, who continued to be connected to the movement, still agreed to meet with me in secret. And it was during these times together, I was able to share with him the impact of my own spiritual journey with Jesus, and the amazing changes He had brought to my life.

It was a couple of years later that my father died. The organization blocked me from going onto his property. Shockingly, the guru communicated to everyone, that my father's death, was due to me leaving the movement! At this point in my life, my heart was experiencing a pain that I knew no cure for. Day after day I felt the weight of grief from the loss of my father, crushing my heart.

This pain stretched from days, into weeks!

HEALING OF ANOTHER KIND

I decided to explore what Jesus said about grief. I knew that healing physical pain was something he did – my own back a testimony! But this pain was different – could he heal that too?

I read from the book of Isaiah where it said this about Jesus…that he was, *"A Man of sorrows and acquainted with grief"*, and *"Surely He has borne our griefs and carried our sorrows"*. (Isaiah 53:3,4 NKJ)

This was the only invitation my heart needed! I decided that the next time I went into a church, I would take my bleeding heart and give it to him on the altar.

And that is exactly what I did! At the end of the next church service I attended, I walked to the front, and said to him, *"I can't handle this grief…you have to take it away!"*

Before I had a chance to repeat my prayer a second time, I felt waves of liquid love pour over my heart, and begin to engulf my deep sadness – it was as if his love pouring in, simply drowned all the grief in one moment of encounter and I felt every weight my heart had carried for weeks, simply lift off me. Tears of joy and gratefulness ran down my face – *I was free!*

The "man of sorrows and acquainted with grief" - *had just healed my broken heart!*

EXILED FROM THE NEW AGE MOVEMENT, MY NEW 'HOME' BECAME MY BMW PARKED BESIDE A BORROWED PUP TENT IN A LOCAL CARAVAN PARK.

The Beginning of the End

[OUT OF THE ASHES]

In the days ahead, I began to take stock of what now felt like the 'left overs' of my past life. At a natural level, it had been decimated into a dozen shattered pieces. However, on another level, I was also experiencing a peace so tangible, that it overshadowed every challenge I was now facing for my future!

I now had a deep internal awareness, that this peace was the result of my decision to follow Jesus with my whole heart!

HOPE ON THE HORIZON

As I sat in the camp ground in my borrowed tent, I began to contemplate my next steps - my heart somehow reassured, that this Jesus who had 'found' me, would also continue to lead me.

It wasn't long before I felt him stirring my heart to leave *all my past behind*, and I knew, this also included my geographical past! I knew that it would mean me moving from Sydney and relocating to Queensland - another state altogether. I also knew that as I made this move, I was taking yet another step forward to follow him. I was now choosing to leave behind me all the memories and the history of almost two decades of my New Age lifestyle in Sydney.

There was nothing in my heart that resisted this gentle invitation from Jesus. Instead, I was aware of a hope growing inside me for a new future, and one I believed that He had planned for me!

A BRAVE NEW WORLD

As I made my move to Queensland, there were two positive and immediate outcomes. The first came in the form of financial provision from a startup business that I had helped run with my Dad before he died.

The second, and more significant, came as I made the choice to learn more about Jesus. I decided that the best place to begin this journey would be to attend a local church.

Remember, that even though I now believed in Jesus as the 'true' Son of God, I was still, at this stage, not your 'typical' Christian convert. I still acted and spoke like a New Ager! I sadly came to realize this truth as I noted time and again, that people in church would choose *not* to sit near me, or what felt even worse, *not* to speak to me. I began to feel strangely and uncomfortably isolated even within the walls of the church.

There is an expression that says, 'You can be lonely, even in a crowd of people!'- I felt this way!

THE HEART OF JESUS

As I bravely tried to navigate my feelings in this new environment, a pastor, aware of my confused and wounded state, offered me a 'lifeline' of hope. He agreed to mentor me through the Bible, and to teach me what it was to be a disciple of Jesus. His mentorship lasted over three years - I received this investment into my life as a timely gift from Jesus.

I had come from a lifestyle of deception and now had a voracious appetite for the truth! I enrolled in Bible College achieving a Diploma in Ministry. Still hungry for more, I continued my studies until I received a Diploma in Theology. I listened, read and studied everything I could about walking with Jesus.

The church had an extensive library filled with books written by men and women who had received powerful truths and life changing revelation from the scriptures. There was also a wall of videos to choose from. Here, I heard stories from the great faith generals, past and present, telling of their dynamic encounters with a supernatural God! I consumed everything I could, aware that every new truth, was powerfully uprooting the foundation of lies from my past.

I knew my life was changing fast – and for the better!

GHOSTS FROM THE PAST

However, during this period of time, there were also some nagging and difficult questions that I knew my heart needed to address:

- *How did I get deceived?*
- *Why did it happen to me?*
- *Why didn't I know?*
- *Why was I deceived for so many years?*

I knew from a place of deep unsettledness, that I would not be able to rest until I found the answers to these painful questions.

As I became more aware of my own journey of revelation, one particular verse from the bible became an 'anchor' for my heart during this season - *"Nevertheless, when one turns to the Lord, the veil is taken away."* 2 Corinthians 3:16 NKJV

This was exactly what I needed to hear as I made my next purposeful steps forward to find a place of resolution for each and every *new* question my heart was now asking…

This was my journey – and a journey I needed to take!

REACH OUT FOR CHRIST – THE CHURCH ON THE GOLD COAST, QUEENSLAND THAT I WAS CONNECTED TO FOR SOME TIME AFTER MY CONVERSION TO CHRISTIANITY

[TRUE ENLIGHTENMENT]

MY PARALLEL JOURNEY

I knew there were deeper levels of truth that Jesus was inviting me to explore with Him. Not only was I seeking definitive answers for the life of deception I had experienced, but there was also another great sadness that lived inside me.

Even though I had now embraced a personal relationship with a living God, and had begun to experience and enjoy the fruit of that connection, my heart still struggled. I knew that I had been personally responsible for leading many others away from a belief in Christ and into a New Age religious lifestyle of deception. I lived with this internal heartache every day.

The verse that challenged me was, *"Do not believe every spirit, but test the spirits, whether they are from God; because many false prophets have gone out into the world."* 1 John 4:1NKJV

I believed that the way for me to move forward, was to find answers that would give me enough evidence to prove the real truth to others - the truth that I had now found! The full intent of my heart was to help them avoid the web of lies that I had so innocently fallen victim to.

With this in mind, I subsequently decided to apply the same research strategies to the New Age movement, as I had done when I was investigating Jesus. I also knew that if I dug deeply enough, and unearthed the origins and the foundations of deception, it would arm me with an arsenal of solid evidence that could prove my case to others.

In making a commitment to this plan, I decided that I would avoid the normal channels of research, i.e., I would *not* reference Christians who wrote about the New Age – I already knew that most of their literature would come with a strong bias of judgement on it.

I also made the choice *not* to read New Age literature, aware that their 'factual' books had taken their teachings from the Bible and twisted them. They made claims that Jesus travelled and lived in India after his resurrection and stated that Catholic priests had later taken this information out of the Bible. I was aware they replaced the word 'resurrection' with the word 'reincarnation' in their writings. They also stated that Constantine was responsible for changing much of the true gospel of Jesus Christ.

AN ARTIST'S IMPRESSION OF A 'HINDU JESUS'

With the above in mind, I decided that my safest and most objective research could only be done in a neutral environment, such as universities and community libraries. I trusted that these were the true 'storehouses' of accurate and historical knowledge within our society.

SHOCK WAVES OF TRUTH

As I began my research, I focused on the study of both Western and Eastern history. I also chose to do a parallel time line search between the Bible and New Age practices. This research spanned over three years of my dedicated time.

In brief, I was able to trace the history and origins of New Age gods and practices throughout different countries, cultures and lineages, including millenniums and centuries. The extent of my research literally spanned a time frame of 3,000 years.

The undeniable truth I discovered shocked me to my core!!

I was able to trace every New Age god and related practice, back to the Old Testament! The names may have been changed as different cultures and countries embraced these false gods, but in essence, these were the identical gods and religious practices that God warned His chosen people to stay away from, calling these practices *idolatry!*

Below is a detailed study from the International Standard Bible Encyclopedia. This comprehensive study traces the historical origins and factual journey of *idolatrous practices* revealed throughout the writings of the Old Testament.

> IDOLATRY = i-dol'-a-tri (teraphim, "household idols," "idolatry"; eidololatreia): There is ever in the human mind a craving for visible forms to express religious conceptions. Idolatry originally meant the worship of idols, or the worship of false gods by means of idols, but came to mean among the Old Testament Hebrews any

worship of false gods, whether by images or otherwise, and finally the worship of Yahweh through visible symbols (Hosea 8:5,6; 10:5); *and ultimately in the New Testament idolatry came to mean, not only the giving to any creature or human creation the honor or devotion which belonged to God alone, but the giving to any human desire a precedence over God's will* (1 Corinthians 10:14; Galatians 5:20; Colossians 3:5; 1 Peter 4:3). *The neighboring gods of Phoenicia, Canaan, Moab--Baal, Melkart, Astarte, Chemosh, Moloch, etc.--were particularly attractive to Jerusalem.. As early as the Assyrian and Babylonian periods (8th and 7th centuries BC), various deities from the Tigris and Euphrates had intruded themselves--the worship of Tammuz becoming a little later the most popular and seductive of all* (Ezekiel 8:14)*--while the worship of the sun, moon, stars and signs of the Zodiac became so intensely fascinating that these were introduced even into the temple itself* (2 Kings 17:16; 21:3-7; 23:4,12; Jeremiah 19:13; Ezekiel 8:16; Amos 5:26).

The special enticements to idolatry as offered by these various cults were found in their deification of natural forces and their appeal to primitive human desires, especially the sexual; also through associations produced by intermarriage and through the appeal to patriotism, when the help of some cruel deity was sought in time of war. Baal and Astarte worship, which was especially attractive, was closely associated with fornication and drunkenness (Amos 2:7,8; compare 1 Kings 14:23), *and also appealed greatly to magic and soothsaying* (e.g. Isaiah 2:6; 3:2; 8:19).

Sacrifices to the idols were offered by fire (Hosea 4:13); *libations were poured out* (Isaiah 57:6; Jeremiah 7:18); *the first-fruits of the earth and tithes were presented* (Hosea 2:8); *tables of food were set before them* (Isaiah 65:11); *the worshippers kissed the idols or threw them kisses* (1 Kings 19:18; Hosea 13:2; Job 31:27); *stretched out their hands in adoration* (Isaiah 44:20); *knelt or prostrated themselves before them and sometimes danced about the altar, gashing themselves with knives* (1 Kings 18:26, 28).

Even earlier than the Babylonian exile the Hebrew prophets taught that Yahweh was not only superior to all other gods, but reigned alone as God, other deities being nonentities (Leviticus 19:4; Isaiah 2:8,18,20; 19:1,3; 31:7; 44:9-20). *The severe satire of this period proves that the former fear of living demons supposed to inhabit the idols had disappeared. These prophets also taught that the temple, ark and sacrifices were not essential to true spiritual worship* (e.g. Jeremiah 3:16; Amos 5:21-25). *These prophecies produced a strong reaction against the previously popular idol-worship, though later indi-*

cations of this worship are not infrequent (Ezekiel 14:1-8; Isaiah 42:17). The Maccabean epoch placed national heroism plainly on the side of the one God, Yahweh; and although Greek and Egyptian idols were worshipped in Gaza and Ascalon and other half-heathen communities clear down to the 5th or 6th century of the Christian era, yet in orthodox centers like Jerusalem these were despised and repudiated utterly from the 2nd century BC onward.

I have literally volumes of documented evidence to support my findings, however, in my next chapter I have highlighted *Mother Nature* as an example of a New Age idolatrous deity that is now effortlessly accepted in our Western society.

Today she is hailed as the female god or goddess responsible for all of creation.

Without going into extensive detail, I have attempted to give an overview of the spiritual lineage and subsequent introduction of this goddess into the Middle East, East Asia and eventually into the West.

[MOTHER NATURE]

MOTHER NATURE JOURNEYS INTO THE MIDDLE EAST 1400 BC

The goddess *Asherah* is introduced, as a consort of El. An Asherah pole or tree stood near Canaanite religious locations to honor this goddess. This was in direct rebellion to God's instruction to His people.

"Do not set up any wooden Asherah pole beside the alter you build to the LORD your God." Deuteronomy 16:21 NKJV

500-600 BC

According to Canaanite mythology, the Mother Goddess deity called Asherah, now has a name change to *Ashtoreth*.

Also against God's command, Solomon chose to marry foreign

wives who brought not only their gods, but the 'spiritual' influence of those gods into his reign.

"But King Solomon loved many foreign women, as well as the daughter of Pharaoh: women of the Moabites, Ammonites, Edomites, Sidonians, and Hittites – from the nations of whom the Lord had said to the children of Israel, "You shall not intermarry with them, nor they with you. Surely they will turn away your hearts after their gods."

Solomon clung to these in love. And he had seven hundred wives, princesses, and three hundred concubines; and his wives turned away his heart. For it was so, when Solomon was old, that his wives turned his heart after other gods; and his heart was not loyal to the Lord his God, as was the heart of his father David. For Solomon went after Ashtoreth the goddess of the Sidonians, and after Milcom the abomination of the Ammonites. Solomon did evil in the sight of the Lord, and did not fully follow the Lord, as did his father David. The Solomon built a high place for Chemosh the abomination of Moab, on the hill that is east of Jerusalem, and for Molech the abomination of the people of Ammon. And he did likewise for all his foreign wives, who burned incense and sacrificed to their gods. And the Lord was angry with Solomon because his heart was turned from the Lord, the God of Israel, Who had appeared to him twice, and had commanded him concerning this thing, that he should not go after other gods, but he did not do what the Lord had commanded." 1 Kings 11:1-10 NKJV

"...because they have forsaken Me, and worshipped Ashtoreth the goddess of the Sidonians" 1 Kings 11:33 NKJV ...remembering these were God's people and descendants of the Canaanites.

A GOOD KING

In 2 Kings 23:13 NKJ, we see King Josiah restoring worship back to God.

"Then the king defiled the high places that were east of Jerusalem, which Solomon king of Israel had built for Ashtoreth the abomination of the Sidonians."

GREEK MYTHOLOGY

The worship of the goddess Ashtoreth now spreads into Cyprus, where she is merged with an ancient Cypriot goddess. This 'merged' goddess may have been adopted into the Greek pantheon in Mycenaean and the times of the Dark Ages to reform as the Greek goddess *Aphrodite.*

In Greek mythology, *Gaia*, also spelled *Gaea*, is the 'personification' of the earth and one of the Greek primordial deities. Gaia is the ancestral mother of all life: the primal Mother Earth goddess.

The earliest written and most reliably dated references to Mother Nature are found in Mycenaean Greek transcripts dated in 12 or 13 BC. The term Mother Earth is transliterated as *'ma-ga'* or *Mother Gaia*.

The personification of Mother Nature was widely popular in the Middle Ages, and as a concept, seated between the properly divine and human, it can be traced to Ancient Greece.

GRECO- ROMAN BC-AD

323 BC TO THE BATTLE OF CORINTH 112 BC - FROM THE DEATH OF ALEXANDER THE GREAT

The Romans call their Mother Earth god, *Tellus Mater* or *Terra Mater,* claiming her as the goddess and creator of the earth.

CONSTANTINE 280-337 AD

Constantine brought Christianity to the Roman Empire. He became the first Western Roman Emperor to profess Christianity and used his power to address the status of Christians, issuing the Edict of Milan in 313. This proclamation legalized Christianity and allowed for freedom of worship throughout the empire. Christianity became the official imperial religion of the Roman Empire, and the first churches were built in England in the second half of the 4th century, overseen by a hierarchy of bishops and priests.

Many existing pagan shrines were converted to Christian use and few pagan sites still operated by the 5th century.

MOTHER NATURE JOURNEYS EAST

1800-1400 BC – THE INDO-ARYAN RACE

The Indo-Aryans migrated into the northern part of South Asia -modern Afghanistan, Bangladesh, India, Pakistan and Nepal.

Both Hinduism and Hindu culture, is believed to have originated from an intermixing or borrowing of Aryan and Dravidian beliefs. They then used these borrowed practices to develop their own distinctive religious beliefs and principles.

The source of Dravidian culture is believed to be from the ancient Indus Civilization, which flourished around 2000 BC.

Members of this civilization worshipped an Earth Goddess similar to the Hindu goddess, *Shakti*.

The traditional line was the same as prevailed amongst the primitive Indus community, which perceived the 'divine female' as Mother Goddess. The Rigveda calls the 'female power' *Mahimata*, a term which literally means Mother Earth.

HINDUISM

The 'divine mother', *Devi Adi Parashakti,* manifests herself in various forms, representing the 'universal creative force'. She becomes Mother Nature *(Mula Prakriti)*, who gives birth to all life forms as plants, animals, etc, from herself, and she sustains and nourishes them through her body, i.e., the earth, animal life, vegetation and minerals. Ultimately it is said that she re-absorbs all life forms back into herself, or devours them to sustain herself – or another way to put it – the power of death, feeding on life - to produce new life. In temples, rituals of puja (worship) are performed daily to this goddess.

Hindu worship of the 'divine Mother' can be traced back to pre-vedic, prehistoric India.

In India today, Hindus show deep reverence to the earth as the Mother Goddess, or sometimes referred to as Mother Earth or The Earth Mother.

Mother Goddess over time has been worshipped by devotional movements and various tantric sects, as the *Divine Mother, Mother of the Universe, Shakti* and *Kali*.

NB: *Kali* is the *Dark Mother Goddess in Hinduism*.

Today, the goddesses *Shakti* and *Kali* have temples that engage in prostitution and sacrifices – the Kalighat Kali Temple is a Hindu temple in West Bengal, India, that is dedicated to the Hindu goddess *Kali*.

600-400 BC BUDDHISM

Buddhism originated in ancient India as a Sramana tradition. In the Southeast Asian Indochina countries of Cambodia, Laos and

Thailand, earth is personified as *Phra Mae Thorani*, the Thai version of Mother Earth, who has her own elevated place in the story of Buddha.

In today's modern Asia culture, the goddess Mother Nature is still worshipped in shrines.

MOTHER NATURE JOURNEYS INTO THE WEST

1800-1900'S

The first recorded use of Mother Nature in English was in 1266 AD, when it was called *'Natura'*. However, the term Mother Goddess was first introduced into Western culture by Hindu gurus, together with the following names for the same deity:

- *Mother Goddess of the Earth*
- *Mother Earth,*
- *Great Mother*
- *Earth Goddess*
- *Mother of The Universe*

Many of these names are now familiar to us all in Western culture. One of the main reasons I chose to highlight this particular deity, was to bring to your awareness the true breadth and often hidden identity of this god. The persona of the 'god' we have embraced in the West is oftentimes, no more than a rather large and jovial 'mother type' figure, sitting atop a mushroom, with a cluster of hundreds of happy children sitting at her feet - innocence, motherly wisdom, virtue and kindness emanating from her lips to her adoring devotees!

The gurus who brought their New Age deception into the West cleverly disguised this Hindu deity to live 'comfortably' amongst our Western culture - the bad fruit of this god's influence subtly woven into the minds and lifestyle of a people, blissfully ignorant to its ulterior dark and deceptive purposes.

The bible gives warning of the subtle strategies the enemy uses to infiltrate our society:

"And no wonder! For Satan himself transforms (masquerades) himself into an angel of light." 2Cor 11:14 NKJV

An excerpt from a recent newspaper article written below, confirms how integrated this particular goddess has become to our Western mindset.

> *"Ahhh summer. It is supposed to be hot in July right? This must be the most normal month we have had all year but I see your social media posts. I see you. You, my friends, are complaining about the heat and to that I say…wait! WHAT? Noooo. You must stop. Mother Nature finally got her act together and you are going to complain? You mustn't anger her. We have seen what she can do. I don't want to see snow in July or live through three season changes in 11 hours."*

The truth is Mother Nature is the exact same goddess *Asherah*, who God warned his people against. Also true is the sinister 'identity' of this foreign god, whose true worship includes prostitution and sacrifice.

In conclusion: the enemy seeks to eradicate from society, both subtly and overtly, the truth that all of creation was brought into existence through the *one and only true God of heaven and earth!*

Genesis 1 confirms that:

In the beginning **God created** *the heavens and the earth.*

God *said, "Let there be light; and there was light."*

God *made the firmament in the midst of the waters.*

God *called the firmament Heaven.*

God *said "Let the waters under the heavens be gathered together in one place, and let the dry land appear.*

God *called the dry land Earth, the waters, He called seas.*

God *created grass, herbs that yield seed, fruit bearing trees.*

God *created two great lights: the sun to rule by day and the moon to rule by night.*

God *created the stars.*

God *created creatures in the sea, birds in the heavens.*

God *created the beasts of the earth, the cattle and every creeping thing on the earth.*

> ***God*** *created man in His own image with the ability to be fruitful and multiply.*
>
> *And God saw everything that He had made, and behold, it was very good and He approved it completely."*

It says of Jesus Christ:

> *In the beginning -before all time was the Word (Christ), and the Word was with God, and the Word was God Himself. He was present originally with God. All things were made and came into existence through Him; and without Him was not even one thing made that has come into being.*
>
> JOHN 1:1-3 NKJV

"He is the image of the invisible God, the firstborn over all creation. For by Him all things were created that are in heaven and that are on earth, visible and invisible, whether thrones or dominions or principalities or powers. All things were created through Him and for Him. And He is before all things, and in Him all things consist."

COLOSSIANS 1:15 NKJV

I rest my case...

AN ARTIST'S IMPRESSION OF A VERY 'WESTERN' MOTHER EARTH

THE ABOVE DESCRIPTION OF MOTHER EARTH IS WHAT WE ARE NOW ACCUSTOMED TO IN OUR WESTERN SOCIETY

[THE GIFT OF TRUTH]

As I continued my in-depth studies, I became more and more aware of the inherent evil that lurked behind the 'personas' of the New Age gods that I had so innocently trusted my life to. Though my Guru had assured me time and again, that there was, *"No such thing as evil"*, my research into the spiritual origins and history of the New Age movement and its gods told me a very different story...

In choosing to parallel my university studies alongside biblical knowledge, the evidence became overwhelming – there was in fact an identified *"...dark ruler of the earthly realm who fills the atmosphere with his authority, and who works diligently in the hearts of those who are disobedient to the truth of God."* Ephesians 2:2 TPT

I felt that another significant piece of the spiritual 'jigsaw puzzle' was beginning to fall into place for me. And I knew I was being drawn into a deeper awareness of the power play that existed in the unseen world of the spirit. My research had begun to validate that there were in fact, *two opposing spiritual forces* at work. Both mandated to target the lives of every man, woman and child on the planet:

- One mandated to bring truth, redemption and eternal life to mankind.
- The other mandated to bring lies, deception and eternal death to mankind.

With this in mind, I made the decision to conclusively search the Bible for every mention of a 'spiritual entity' identified as evil. As I did so, I discovered that the Bible uses several names for this 'entity': *the evil one, the devil, satan, beelzebub (lord of the flies) lucifer, the angel of light, the dragon, the serpent,* and many more.

In sharing my findings with you, I am also aware in our scientific, rational age, that spiritual beliefs are often scorned as 'myths' and that many would rather believe human theory than accept divine revelation. As I lived over two decades of my life spiritually deceived and naively on a path to self destruction and eternal separation from God, I am therefore unwavering in my commitment to reveal the light of truth whenever I find it. In having said that, my heart, however, is in no way wanting to glorify the enemy, but rather bring an educated awareness that - *we do in fact, have an enemy!*

THE DEVIL IS BIBLE FACT AND PRESENT DAY REALITY

It has always been the devil's cleverest ruse to make mankind believe that he doesn't exist and to pull the veil of darkness over his kingdom so we won't understand who he is. By 'masking' himself he can tempt and deceive people without blame!

As I studied the scriptures, I noted that Jesus taught His disciples to pray specifically to His Father for their protection against the enemy: *"And do not lead us into temptation, But deliver us from the evil one. For Yours is the kingdom and the power and the glory forever."* Matthew 6:13 NKJV

We can see clearly from this verse that the 'evil one' was not simply a figment of Jesus' imagination – he was a real spiritual entity.

- Jesus also calls him, *"the ruler of this world"* John 12:31 NKJV
- The Pharisees call him, *"Beelzebub, the prince of demons"* Matthew 12:24 NKJV
- Paul calls him, *"the god of this age"* 2 Corinthians 4:4 NKV and *"the prince of the power of the air"* Ephesians 2:2 NKV

To clarify, regardless of what 'name' he is called - he is not on equal footing with God!

THE DEVIL'S M.O.

Below is a list, though not exhaustive, of some of the more distinctive DNA characteristics of the enemy and his mode of operation. The quotes from Jesus give us the greatest clarification.

HE IS THE FATHER OF LIES

Jesus speaking: *"He was a murderer from the beginning, and does not stand in the truth, because there is no truth in him. When he speaks a lie, he speaks what is natural to him, for he is a liar himself and the father of lies and all that is false."* John 8:44 AMPC

HE IS THE THIEF

Again Jesus speaking: *"Most assuredly, I say to you, he who does not enter the sheepfold by the door, but climbs up some other way, the same is a thief and a robber.*

He goes on to say: *"Most assuredly I say to you, I am the door of the sheep. All who ever came before Me are thieves and robbers, but the sheep did not hear them. I am the door. If anyone enters by Me, he will be saved, and will go in and out and find pasture. The thief does not come except to steal, and to kill, and to destroy. I have come that they may have life and life more abundantly."* John 10:1, 7-10 NKJV

HE IS THE DEVOURER

Satan compels or entices his prey to follow him whether they realize it or not – whether they are ignorant, confused, blind, bound or willing – he doesn't care. However, the Bible gives us clear warning of his tactics…

The Apostle Paul writes, *"…that we would not be exploited by the adversary Satan for we know his clever schemes."* 2 Corinthians 2:11 TPT

"Be well balanced and always alert, because your enemy, the devil, roams around incessantly, like a roaring lion looking for its prey to devour." 1 Peter 5:8 TPT

The Amplified Bible says it this way, *"…for that enemy of yours, the devil, roams around like a lion roaring in fierce hunger, seeking someone to seize upon and devour."*

HE IS THE TEMPTER

"Then Jesus was led up by the Spirit into the wilderness to be tempted by the devil. And when he had fasted 40 days and nights, afterward He was hungry. Now when the tempter came to Him, he said, "If You are the son of God, command that these stones become bread."

At the end of all the devil's temptations in the wilderness, Jesus tells him, *"It is written again, you shall not tempt the Lord your God."* Matthew 4:3,7 NKJ

In this one great statement, Jesus is clarifying the devil's position as a 'subordinate' to God!

"Let no one say when he is tempted 'I am tempted by God'; for God cannot be tempted by evil, nor does He Himself tempt anyone." James 1:13 NKJV

The scriptures also tell us that Jesus, *"... suffered and endured every test and temptation, so that He can help us every time we pass through the ordeals of life."* Hebrews 2:18 TPT

Again, the above verses amplify the undeniably disparate differences between the enemy's evil intent and God's plan of salvation for mankind, in every circumstance of life.

HE IS THE ACCUSER

The word 'devil' comes from the Greek word *diabolos*. It means slanderer or false accuser.

"Now is come salvation, and strength, and the kingdom of our God, and the power of His Christ: for the accuser of our brethren is cast down, which accused them before our God day and night." Revelation 12:10 NKJV

It is part of the devil's work in our lives to bring accusation and lies against us – robbing us of confidence before God and negating the promise of His forgiveness. The truth is, when Christ died, every accusation of the enemy was nullified. *He can never separate us from the love of God in Christ Jesus.*

HE IS THE ANGEL OF LIGHT

The very name *Lucifer* means 'lightbearer'.

The Apostle Paul in the book of Corinthians laments the presence of false teachers who appeared in the early church, saying: *"And no wonder! For Satan himself transforms himself into an angel of light."* 2 Corinthians 11:14 NKJV

The Bible refers to an 'angel of light' as one of the devil's fallen angelic 'angels', who deceptively clothes itself with 'light' to hide its true and evil identity.

I can verify the above as fact. As a practicing leader in the New Age movement, I was accustomed to 'angels of light' visiting me. When they appeared, I would see them with my natural eyes. We would converse together and they would give me their 'wisdom'. Because they were clothed in light, I thought they were spiritual beings who had been assigned to help direct my life.

I learnt later that another notable New Age leader, Randall Baer, had similar 'angels of light' visit him. He became famous for his insights into the strange new phenomena of 'crystals' that had begun to sweep the world. He was regarded as the Guru and his book became the 'bible' of everything crystal.

Randall built a pyramid in his own backyard, where he said 'angels of light' would visit him, telling him all about crystals, their energy force and the powers they contained.

Randall tells the remarkable story of what happened to him when he found out that a group of Christians had begun to pray for him. Their prayer was that the 'angels of light' would be exposed to him and seen for who they truly were.

Their prayers were answered! One day as he sat inside his pyramid the 'angels of light' appeared. However, what happened next, Randall was in no way prepared for – as he watched the 'angels', the translucent light that they were shrouded in, began to disappear before his eyes. As it did so, he started to see the forms of grotesque and dark 'beings' appear in their place. He realized that he was now looking at the personification of evil itself.

He was so frightened by this encounter, he literally ran from the pyramid, and straight into the nearest church, where he gave his heart and life to Jesus!

He continued to speak at his seminars, now carrying the message of true enlightenment through Jesus Christ – his New Age attendees left his meetings in droves. Unable to pull his book on crystals from the shelves of stores, he added an appendix, exposing and denouncing the devil's plans behind the whole crystal movement worldwide.

"But whenever a person turns in repentance to the Lord, the veil is stripped off and taken away. Now the Lord is the Spirit, and where the Spirit of the Lord is, there is freedom – emancipation from bondage, freedom." 2 Corinthians 3:16,17 AMPC

Both Randall and I as New Age leaders, had similar extraordinary experiences encountering Jesus for the first time. For us both, it will always have to be said, that it was nothing short of a miracle!

In a divinely orchestrated moment of time, Jesus removed the 'veil' of deception from our lives, and we were born again into a completely different kingdom – *His Kingdom of true light!*.

Colossians 1:13 TPT says it perfectly, *"He has rescued us completely from the tyrannical rule of darkness and has translated us into the kingdom realm of His beloved Son."*

HE IS THE GREAT DECEIVER

"For the god of this world has blinded the unbelievers' minds that they should not discern the truth, preventing them from seeing the illuminating light of the Gospel of the glory of Christ the Messiah, Who is the image and likeness of God." 2 Corinthians 4:4 AMPC

For me, every moment of exhaustive research and study that had spanned the last three years of my life, culminated in the truth contained in this one single verse above.

I was at last able to give full identification to the 'evil entity' that had so cruelly and intentionally imprisoned my life for almost two decades – it was the one the Bible calls The Great Deceiver!

The Dictionary Definition of the word *deceiver* means:

To mislead by deliberate misrepresentation or lies, delude, lead

astray, imposing a false belief that causes ignorance, bewilderment or helplessness.

The above definition so perfectly described my New Age journey!

Jesus quotes these words when speaking of The Deceiver:

You are the offspring of your father, the devil, and you serve your father very well, passionately carrying out his desires. He's been a murderer right from the start! He never stood with the truth, for he's full of nothing but lies – lying is his native tongue. He is the mater of deception and the father of lies!" John 8:44 TPT

Military leaders will tell you – in any battle, one of the single greatest 'keys' to their victory, is to understand their enemy. The enemy also knows if their opponent doesn't understand or recognize him, they won't initiate any strategies necessary to ensure their win and the enemy's subsequent defeat.

It is an identical strategy when it comes to winning battles in the realm of the spirit!

As my studies throughout the Bible had now confirmed the existence of the devil, I now had a slew of other questions I needed answers to –

- *Where did the devil come from?*
- *What was his origin?*
- *When did he appear?*
- *When and why did he begin his evil assignment agains Mankind?*

RANDALL BAER'S EARLIER BOOKS EXTOLLING THE
VIRTUES AND HIDDEN POWERS OF CRYSTALS

RANDALL'S BOOK AFTER HIS CONVERSION TO
CHRISTIANITY HE DENOUNCED THE NEW AGE, WARNING
OF ITS DANGERS AND EVIL INTENT

12

[WHEN EVIL TOOK CENTRE STAGE]

I knew instinctively that the answers I was looking for had to come from the one absolute source of truth and wisdom for my life, and that was the Bible.

In taking you on this journey through the scriptures with me, my aim is to provide you with a clearer understanding of the events that took place at the beginning of the earth's creation. I am also hopeful that it will offer you more knowledge and give you greater 'context' for the spiritual power play that is at work on the earth today.

With this in mind, my starting point is in the book of Genesis, the first book of the Bible. It gives us a full and detailed account of the beginning of creation.

THE BIRTHPLACE OF CREATION

When God finished creating the heavens and the earth, the bible says, *"And God saw that it was good."* Genesis 1:25 NKJV

Then God said, "Let Us make man in Our image, according to Our likeness..." So God created man in His own image, in the image of God He created him; male and female He created them. Then God blessed them, and God said to them, "Be fruitful and multiply; fill the earth and subdue it; have dominion..."

"Then God saw everything that He had made, and indeed it was very good." Genesis 1:26-28,v31 NKJV

So this now leaves me asking the question...

If *everything* in the beginning that God created was good and very good, then where and when did evil first make its appearance to malign God's perfect creation - when God Himself didn't create anything evil?

Again, the Bible gives us clear answers.

THE INSURRECTION OF SATAN

Between the perfection of creation described in Genesis 1:31, *"Behold, it was very good."* and the appearance of evil in Genesis 3, something happened...

The Bible references an angel called *Lucifer*, which literally means 'morning star' and it says of him:

"You were in Eden, the garden of God. Your clothing was adorned with every precious stone – red carnelian, pale green peridot, white moonstone, blue-green beryl, onyx, green jasper, blue *lapis lazuli*, turquoise, and emerald – all beautifully crafted for you and set in the finest gold. They were given to you on the day you were created. I ordained and anointed you as the mighty angelic guardian. You had access to the holy mountain of God and walked among the stones of fire."

The Bible then goes on to say:

"You were blameless in all you did from the day you were created until the day evil was found in you." Ezekiel 28:13-15 NKJV

These texts give us conclusive evidence that Lucifer was the 'anointed cherub' who was given Heaven's high office. This position came with authority and responsibility to protect and defend the holy mountain of God. The high order and specific placement of Lucifer prior to his fall afforded him the unique opportunity to bring glory to God, including leading Heaven's choirs in the worship of The Most High.

Isaiah 14:12-15 then gives us an account of Lucifer's fall:

"How you are fallen from heaven, O Lucifer, son of the morning! How you are cut down to the ground, ("You have been cast down to the earth") You who weakened the nations! For you have said in your heart:

I will ascend into heaven,

I will exalt my throne above the stars of God;

I will sit on the mount of the congregation on the farthest sides of the north;

I will ascend above the heights of the clouds,

I will be like the Most High."

Verse 17 then tells us, *"Your heart became proud on account of your beauty, and you corrupted your wisdom because of your splendor."*

From these texts, we see that Lucifer went from being an anointed angelic guardian, to becoming the *embodiment of evil*. He turned his eyes away from his Creator to himself. He became proud and *a desire to rule* was born in him. He whispered his lies until one third of the angelic host of heaven sided with him!

"And war broke out in heaven: Michael and his angels fought with the dragon; and the dragon and his angels fought, but they did not prevail, nor was a place found for them in heaven any longer. So the great dragon was cast out, that serpent of old, called the devil and satan, who deceives the whole world; he was cast to the earth, and his angels were cast out with him." Revelation 12:7-9 NKJV

It is very clear from the above verses that the devil and his hoard of fallen 'angels' were cast out of heaven and onto the earth. The devil's 'new' mission, *"to deceive the whole world"* Revelation 12:9 NKJV, and to set himself up as *"the ruler of this world"* John 12:31 NKJV, and *"the god of this age".* 2 Corinthians 4:4 NKJV

The Bible teaches us that the devil rules over *"all the kingdoms of the inhabited earth"*, and therefore does not dwell in any one physical location on the earth but is confined to the vicinity of the earth! (Luke 4:5,6 NKJV)

This is the 'one' we now meet in Genesis 3. The book of Revelation calls him, *"that ancient serpent"*.

He is already evil, already a deceiver and already a murderer, when he appears in the garden of God as *"the serpent"*.

It says of the devil that, *"He was more cunning than any beast of the field which the Lord God made."* Genesis 3:1 NKJV

The very first thing he does as he speaks to Eve, is call God's word into question, *"Did God actually say, 'You shall not eat of every tree in the garden?'"*

And the woman said to the serpent, "We may eat the fruit of the trees of the garden; but of the fruit of the tree which is in the midst of the garden, God has said, 'You shall not eat it, nor shall you touch it, lest you die.'"

Then the serpent said to the woman, "You will not surely die. For God knows that in the day you eat of it your eyes will be opened, and you will be like God, knowing good and evil." Genesis 3:2-5 NKJV

We all know how that ended! Eve succumbed to the temptation, took the fruit, ate it and then gave it to her husband!

THE POWER SHIFT

God had given Adam the dominion and authority of this world. In this one act of disobedience, he committed *high treason* and gave his God designated authority into the hands of the devil.

Who gave the devil authority? God's created man Adam!

To put it bluntly, when Adam sinned, he put us all in the 'pawn shop'! To get out you need a redeeming ticket. And God knew there would not be enough money in the universe to buy us out.

The only 'redeeming ticket' to save mankind, would be the death of His own Son - a sinless sacrifice that was powerful enough to buy man back into a personal relationship with his Creator and Holy God.

I've heard a minister put it this way, *"The Son of God became a man, so the sons of men could become the sons of God!"*

When Jesus rose from the dead, He took back His authority from the devil, and delegated it to every born again believer on the planet. This also meant that He was reinstating mankind back into his original rulership position – he was now able to once more, exercise his dominion and take authority over the devil - *"the ruler of this world"*. John 12:31 NKJV

The devil is the oppressor and author of hatred against all human kind. Sickness, disease, oppression and fear is his will!

To quote the words of Jesus, *"The thief does not come except to steal, and to kill, and to destroy. I have come that they may have life, and that they may have it more abundantly."* John 10:10 NKJV

Jesus is our Deliverer, and the will of God in human form, *"Who went about doing good, and healing all who were oppressed by the devil because God was with Him."* Acts 10:38 NKJV

If we therefore, believe that God is the author of any form of evil on the planet, i.e., sickness, disease, poverty, oppression or calamity etc., *then we ourselves have been deceived by The Deceiver!*

God is a God of love!

The devil is the lowest form of spiritual being on the planet today.

CHANGE OF OWNERSHIP

When Adam and Eve ate from *"the tree of the knowledge of good and evil"*, they didn't just disobey God, they obeyed the devil. God had told them, *"You shall not eat, for in the day that you eat of it you shall surely die."* Genesis 2:17 NKJV

In this one single act of disobedience, Adam and Eve changed masters. They committed *high treason* and gave their delegated authority into the hands of the devil!

In Luke chapter 4, we read that Jesus was *"led into the wilderness, being tempted for 40 days by the devil."*

It goes on to say, *"Then the devil, taking Him up on a high mountain, showed Him all the kingdoms of the world in a moment of time. And the devil said to Him, "All this authority I will give You, and their glory; for this has been delivered to me, and I give it to whomever I wish."* v 1, 5,6 NKJV

We can clearly see from the above verses that the devil states that he had been given the authority and therefore, 'legal' ownership of *"all the kingdoms of this world"*!

REPOSITIONED TO RULE

However, when Jesus rose from the dead, He made this statement, *"All authority has been given to Me in heaven and on earth."* Matthew 28:1 NKJV

How and when did Jesus take back His authority from the devil?

Again the scriptures give us full insight. We read in the book of Ephesians that when Christ died, He *"...first decended into the lower parts of the earth (hell itself),* and *"When He ascended on high (rose from the dead), He led captivity captive, a train of vanquished foes..."* Ephesians 4:8,9 AMPC

And further that, *"God disarmed the principalities and powers that were ranged against us and made a bold display and public example of them, in triumphing over them in Him (Jesus) and in the cross."* Colossians 2:15 AMPC

The scriptures also tell us that when God raised Jesus from the dead, He *"Seated Him at His right hand in the heavenly places, far above all principality and power and might and dominion, and every name that is named, not only in this age but also in that which is to come. And He put all things under His feet, and gave Him to be the head over all things to the church, which is His body, the fullness of Him who fills all in all."* Ephesians 1:20-23 NKJV

HEAVENLY PLACES

I believe one of the most critical insights that will also help us gain an understanding of our 'positional authority' in Christ Jesus, is to also have knowledge of the 'three heavens' that the Bible speaks of.

THE FIRST HEAVEN

The 'first heaven' is the visible kingdom – it is the world we live in and are most aware of. It is this visible kingdom that Genesis 1 speaks of. It includes the earth, the seas, the sun, the moon and stars, all plant life bearing seeds, the fish, birds, cattle and beasts of the field.

THE SECOND HEAVEN

The 'second heaven' is an unseen spiritual realm just above the earth where the devil and his fallen angels rule.

Remember in the book of Revelation 12:7-9 NKJV, that it states, *"the devil...who deceives the whole world: he was cast to the earth, and his angels were cast out with him."*

Ephesians chapter 6 gives us greater insight into the 'second heaven', when it instructs us to:

"Put on God's whole armor, that you may be able successfully to stand up against all the strategies and the deceits of the devil. For we are not wrestling with flesh and blood (contending only with physical opponents), but against the despotisms, against the powers, against (the master spirits who are) the world rulers of this present darkness, against the spirit forces of wickedness in the heavenly sphere (places)." Ephesians 6:10-12 AMPC

We also read in Ephesians 2:2 NKJV, *"...in which you once walked according to the course of this world, according to the prince of the power of the air, the spirit who now works in the sons of disobedience."*

The *"power of the air"* is clearly inferred to be the devil's realm. This is his legal place of habitation and his spiritual 'head quarters'. It is from the second heaven that he and his demonic 'angels' unleash their tidal wave of *"spiritual wickedness"* onto the earth. He has been given authority to rule from this realm.

Today, we all witnesses to the uncontrollable slew of "viral terrorism" that is assailing mankind, through every possible airway and access point across our planet. Where once the 'face of evil' was subtly hidden behind closed doors, it now struts shamelessly and aggressively through the massive technological advancements of our age. The devil, whose seat of power is from the second heaven, controls the airways, and delivers, en masse, the voice of fear, oppression and terror, to all mankind. Where once our children's lives were protected by the safety of silence, the voice of the enemy now marches defiantly into our homes, our schools and every communication infrastructure of our modern society.

THE THIRD HEAVEN

In 2 Corinthians 2:12 AMPC, Paul tells us, *"I know a man in Christ who 14 years ago – whether in the body or out of the body I do not know, God knows – was caught up to the third heaven."*

The 'third' heaven is where God and His angels dwell. It is also where Christ is now seated at the right hand of His Father, *"Whereas this One, Christ, after He had offered a single sacrifice for our sins for all time, sat down at the right hand of God."* Hebrews 10:12 AMPC

"...and seated Him at His right hand in the heavenly places." Ephesians 1:20 NKJV

THE ANGELS OF THE THIRD HEAVEN

To recap, one third of the angels were cast out of heaven to the earth as a result of the devil's revolt.

The scriptures give us insight into the 'job description' of the remaining two thirds of the angels who remain in the third heaven with God.

"Referring to the angels He says, God Who makes His angels winds and His ministering servants flames of fire." Hebrews 1:7 NKJV

The Amplified Bible says it this way, *"Are not the angels all ministering spirits (servants) sent out in the service of God for the assistance of those who are to inherit salvation?"*

Matthew 4:11 NKJV tells us angels ministered to Jesus after His temptation in the wilderness, *"Then the devil departed from Him, and behold, angels came and ministered to Him."*

There are countless incidents cited in scripture where *ministering angels* were deployed by God from the third heaven, to carry out specific assignments on the earth. These angels still remain on heavenly assignment today!

"Bless the Lord, you His angels, who excel in strength, who do His word, heeding the voice of His word.

Bless the Lord, all you His hosts, you ministers of His, who do His pleasure." Psalm 103:20 NKJV

There are no demons or principalities in the third heaven!

THE AUTHORITY OF THE BELIEVER

The devil had authority because Adam gave it to him!

Jesus died as a sinless 'man', so He could take legal authority back from the devil.

Who did Jesus give His authority back to?

He gave it to every man, woman and child on the planet, who choose to make Jesus the Lord of their life.

"Listen carefully: I have given you authority (that you now possess) to tread on serpents and scorpions, and (the ability to exercise authority) over all the power of the enemy (satan); and nothing will (in any way) harm you." Luke 10:19 AMPC

The same authority that is in Christ now lives in the believer - this is the foundation of Christianity!

When we make Jesus the Lord of our lives, we are immediately, "... raised up together, and made to sit together in the heavenly places in Christ Jesus..." Ephesians 2:6 NKJV

This means, that as human beings, we live in the *first heaven*, but as 'born again' humans, we also live in the *third heaven!*

Why is this so important?

As born again believers, we can choose to *only live in the first heaven*. However, this choice is a dangerous one!

Even though the second heaven has been disarmed, and the authority has been delegated back to followers of Christ, the *second heaven* will continue to have rulership over an individual until they *take up their positional authority from the third heaven.*

To put it simply - if we don't take our rightful position in the third heaven, *the enemy will determine our future from the second heaven* - and the outcomes of our lives will look very different...!

THE GOD OF SELF

As a follow on from biblical research, I wanted to conclude this chapter by bringing one of the most major deceptions of the New Age, to the forefront - the *gospel of self!*

The New Age movement believes conclusively, that god is not *in you,* but that *you are god!*

The focus on 'self' and *you* as a god comes from the Hindu religion. A greeting that we have become all too familiar with in the West, *Namaste* actually translates to, *"I bow to the divine in you"*, acknowledging the god inside of you, and that *you are god!*

When I was a leader in the New Age and running Personal and Professional Development Seminars for thousands of participants, we put a strong emphasis on the spiritual authority of 'self'.

Sadly, I watched this deceptive belief system play out with dire consequences in people's lives. I saw spouses leave one another, their children, their jobs and have affairs. Basically, the premise we taught was, *"If you want to do it and it's good for you, then it's all ok."*, and because 'self' was now the focus, it didn't matter who got hurt!

Our goal was to strip people's old belief systems down. This included taking accountability, caring for others and taking any responsibility for their own lives or tragically, the lives of others

We also undermined their search for an external God!

We would re-teach them that 'self' was the most important spiritual focus affirming, that they are, in fact, gods!

Does this sound at all familiar? It is the complete MO of the devil, who set himself on a course of self exaltation and presumed self determination - defiantly unwilling to become a subordinate to his God!

The ultimate goal of the enemy's deceptive strategy behind the New Age emphasis on 'self as god', is to completely destroy the idea that there are any consequences for man's sin. And therefore, if there are no consequences, then that would completely eradicate man's need for a Savior.

A deadly end result for all mankind!

THE GOD OF LOVE

However, the Bible teaches otherwise –

"For all have sinned and fall short of the glory of God." Romans 3:23 NKJV

When Adam disobeyed God in the garden his sin carried with it a penalty for all mankind...

"For the wages of sin is death, but the gift of God is eternal life in Christ Jesus our Lord." Romans 6:23 NKJV

Because of God's unrequited love for His most magnificent creation, He could not bear to leave mankind eternally separated from Himself, so He did the unthinkable:

"For God so loved the world that He gave His only begotten Son, that whoever believes in Him should not perish but have everlasting life. For God did not send His Son into the world to condemn the world, but that the world through Him might be saved." John 3:16,17 NKJV

"Even when we were dead and doomed in our many sins, He united us into the very life of Christ and saved us by His wonderful grace!" Ephesians 2:5 TPT

THE SIN QUESTION TODAY

I recently heard a young minister speak on his keen observation of our current Christian culture and their approach to the subject of sin.

He observed that 'secular thought' is now taking over some areas of church culture, and is stronger than biblical thought. He shared his insights on how this is affecting whole people groups and their approach to personal accountability for sin.

He quotes a practicing clinical psychologist/psychiatrist who deals with broken people who made this statement:

"If sin is not in their vocabulary, I cannot help them!" - this man is not a believer.

The minister went on to say:

> *"One of the byproducts of a secular mindset is that sin becomes a 'non conversation'! God's Word itself begins to leave our understanding, our conscience and our vocabulary, because we have now found ways to justify every action we've done. We have evidence! We have proof! We have a group of people that believe the same way we do! We follow them, we get around them and we justify our action...we now have found so many ways to talk ourselves out of conviction! We butter it up a little differently, just to make ourselves feel better. Today, we find ways 'out', such as, "I didn't mean that", "I'm good", etc, etc. We've become too knowledgeable for our own good and we no longer respond to the promptings of the Holy Spirit who was sent to, "...convict the world of sin" and "...guide you into all truth..." (John 16:8,13 NKJV)*

He wraps up his observations with this powerful conclusion:

> *"Guess what, if you continue to avoid the conviction of God, the Holy Spirit... you're going to end up with a completely 'secular world view' and you'll become your own god...and the moment someone removes the concept of sin, is the moment we remove the need for God... and we become our own god!"*

How sadly familiar does this sound in the light of what we now know is the devil's objective in the lives of mankind today:

- *To remove man's need for a Savior*
- *To remove the deity of Jesus*

"SO THE GREAT DRAGON WAS CAST OUT, THAT SERPENT OF OLD, CALLED THE DEVIL AND SATAN, WHO DECEIVES THE WHOLE WORLD, HE WAS CAST TO THE EARTH, AND HIS ANGELS WERE CAST OUT WITH HIM." REVELATION 12:9 NKJV

13

[SLEEPING WITH THE ENEMY]

In this next chapter, I want to take a more serious look at the significant increase of New Age practices, both within our Western culture, and more alarmingly, within our Christian culture at large.

I clearly remember as a leader in the New Age, we had planned meetings to develop strategies to 'convert' Christians by inaugurating, or drip feeding them, towards our philosophies and belief systems. We planned to strategically 'wean' them over a 30 year period of time, believing this time frame, would be long enough to create a substantial 'foothold' into the Christian culture of the day.

We are around that 30 year mark now!

The statistics below are quoted from a recent survey compiled by the US Pew Research Centre:

U.S. adults who identify as Christians are just as likely as the religiously unaffiliated, and the population as a whole, to hold New Age beliefs, according to a recent report from Pew Research Center.

About 6 in 10 Americans overall (62 percent) hold at least one of the four New Age beliefs included in the survey: belief that spiritual energy can be located in physical things, such as mountains and trees; belief in psychics; belief in reincarnation; and belief in astrology. The share was virtually the same among Christians (61 percent).

Forty percent of both Christians and "nones" affirmed belief in psychics, while roughly one-quarter of Christians and 32 percent of the unaffiliated said they believe in astrology. On the question of reincarnation, 29 percent of Christians and 38 percent of the unaffiliated claimed this New Age belief. And 37 percent of Christians expressed belief in spiritual energy inhabiting physical things.

While evangelicals were the least likely of any group to subscribe to New Age beliefs, nearly half (47 percent) of evangelical respondents nevertheless claimed at least one.

As a response to the Pew Survey, The Gospel Coalition makes the below observation:

> *Religious syncretism is the blending of two or more religious belief systems into a new system, or the incorporation into a religious tradition of beliefs from unrelated traditions. In the era of American's founding, a dominant strain—especially popular among the Founding Fathers, like George Washington and Thomas Jefferson—was "Christian deism." In our own day, syncretism often mixes Christian beliefs with secular philosophy, such as in the form of Moralistic Therapeutic Deism. But the Pew Research survey shows an unexpected form of syncretism has crept into our culture and into our churches.*
>
> *We tend to assume people intuitively understand why a belief in the God who revealed himself in the Bible and in Christ is incompatible with a belief in reincarnation or the healing power of crystals. Because of this assumption, we spend almost no time explaining to our fellow churchgoers why New Age and Christian beliefs are incompatible. The result is that many people in our churches have a malfunctioning plausibility structure.*
>
> *Everything we believe is filtered through our plausibility structures—a belief-forming apparatus that acts as a gatekeeper, letting in evidence matched against what we*

already consider to be possible. Plausibility structures filter out claims that we believe cannot be reasonable or potentially true. They don't necessarily tell us if a claim is true, only that the truth of the claim appears plausible enough for us to accept and that we are not wholly unwarranted in thinking it could be true. Whether we are gullible or skeptical, the beliefs we accumulate have been filtered through plausibility structures at the individual and cultural level. These eventually form our worldview, which itself becomes a broad strainer that filters out beliefs that we won't even consider to be possibly true.

Plausibility structures can prevent people from forming beliefs inconsistent with experience, evidence, and a Christian worldview. But these structures have to be built upon solid biblical teaching, rather than just assumed to have been acquired through church culture.

DANGEROUS LIAISONS

As I processed the above survey results, it sadly confirmed my belief that an *alternative culture* has been emerging for some time within Christendom and the church worldwide. I define it as 'New Age Christianity' – a name I believe, that identifies the DNA of a new wave of 'believers' spread across the planet, who still stubbornly defend their position calling themselves *"followers of Jesus"*.

As a result of my background, I inherently know firsthand the gravity and implications of practicing New Age beliefs as a 'born again' Christian, and to be honest, it has never been the easiest of tasks to communicate my concerns with any Christian engaged in such practices. I have tried on many occasions, only to end up in heated disagreements. I also know that the defensiveness I have encountered time and again is 'spiritual' in its' origin.

The single greatest motivation of my heart in writing this book has been to bring 'evidence that demands a verdict' into today's Christian culture. My greatest hope is to bring insight and help to those who are innocently exposed to the current slew of new and dangerous forms of deceit currently available in today's 'spiritual market'! My desire is that the knowledge I share will equip them to recognize the lies of the enemy, and, in so doing, enable them to redirect their lives towards the safety of truth.

The undeniable fact is that New Age practices have now become the accepted 'norm' to an entire generation of believers!

With the above information at the forefront of my mind, I knew I needed God's perspective to enable me to effectively communicate to others. I wanted to come from a position of truth and clarity, yet without any emotion or judgement.

God gave me exactly that in one powerful, yet simple 'aha moment' of insight!

DIVINE PERSPECTIVE

He spoke to my heart about my marriage to my beautiful wife, Anne-Marie. He showed me that when I was unmarried, I was *free to date whoever I wanted to*, but the moment I entered into the Covenant of Marriage with her, my life and every part of it now belonged to her, and her alone!

Even my body did not belong to me anymore – it belonged to my wife! The Covenant of Marriage means that "*the two now become one flesh*", so whatever I choose or not choose to do with my body, ultimately will affect her life, i.e., if I eat poorly and run it into the ground, then she will reap the consequences of my bad choices. This means that I now have a responsibility to care for myself for her sake. It also means that I now choose to lay down *what gratifies me* because of my love for her - when I want to, and when I don't want to.

It's called a sacrifice for love!

It is ultimately the same with Jesus! When I made Him the Lord of my life, I made Him Lord of every part of me, including my body. My body now belongs to Him, and because I am aware of the impact of this truth, I choose to keep it holy for God's presence alone. If I were to give my body, that is now in a Covenant relationship with God, to New Age practices, I would be guilty of allowing other gods to have access, not only to my physical body, but to every other part of my world…

"Do you not know that your body is the temple (the very sanctuary) of the Holy spirit Who lives within you, Whom you have received as a Gift from God? You are not your own..." 1 Corinthians 6:19 AMPC

GROUNDS FOR DIVORCE

Probably the single greatest argument that 'believers' present to me who are engaged in New Age practices, is this:

"As long as I'm thinking about Jesus while I'm doing it, it's ok!"

However, this argument doesn't hold any validity when it comes to a relationship based on Covenant truth.

A parallel argument I could use as Anne-Marie's husband would be:

"It's ok for me to date, kiss or even sleep with other women, as long as I'm thinking about Anne-Marie while I'm doing it!"

If I were to engage in *any* New Age practice as a Christian, it would be the same as me choosing to give myself to other women *while married to Anne-Marie!* Quite simply, I would be breaking the Covenant of our Marriage.

There is no 'nice' way to put it – it's called Adultery!

The same is true of my relationship with Jesus! To continue with any New Age practice in my life as a born again believer, means that I would literally have to go back through the cross of Jesus and break my Covenant with Him as my Lord and Savior. This would amount to me placing myself once more under the control and dominion of the 'lords' who had authority and legislation of my life pre Christ.

The cross was the point of no return to my past life!

When the bible told me that *"I had become a new creation in Christ Jesus"*, that meant that the 'old' Alan literally died to everything that held me captive, and I was raised to a brand new life in Christ. My old life was now dead and buried - it no longer existed! This meant that there was now absolutely *no contest* for my heart to leave the safety of truth and re-engage in *any* former practice that was attached to the lies and deception of my past life.

To do so, I would be guilty of what the bible calls Idolatry!

Idolatry is the worship of false gods in a visible form whether by images or otherwise. *Adultery* is oftentimes mentioned in scripture next to Idolatry.

- *Idolatry is in the Spirit, what adultery is in the flesh and both are a betrayal of devotion!*

"Therefore if any person is ingrafted in Christ the Messiah he is a new creation (a new creature altogether); the old previous moral and spiritual condition has passed away. Behold the fresh and new has come!" 2 Corinthians 5:17 AMPC

Below is the clearest illustration I can give you of this truth:

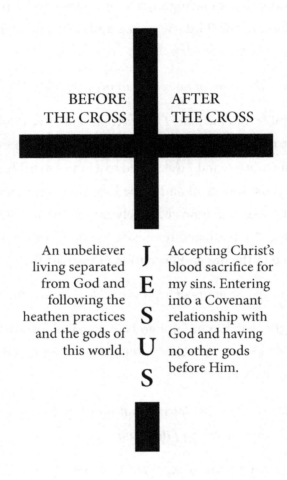

THE GRAVITY OF COVENANT LOVE

There is another great anchor for my heart in turning away from heathen practices and it's not simply because God tells me not to - *it's because of love!* I have experienced over and over again the overwhelming grace and forgiveness of a perfect Father who has covenanted Himself to me in love. I spent countless years of my life hating Him and turning others away from His heart – and yet He relentlessly pursued me until the day I yielded my life to Him.

I finally found a God who wanted a deeply personal and loving relationship with me!

I continued to find powerful truths throughout His word on the depth of intimacy and encounter He was offering to my heart. When Jesus rose from the dead and interacted with Mary in the garden, His instruction to her was to tell the others, *"Go to My brethren and tell them, I am ascending to My Father and your Father, and to My God and your God."* John 20:17 NKJV

Jesus' death had secured my invitation into a lifestyle of intimacy with the Father's heart – I had become His son and part of God's family. The bible declares, *"For the same love He has for His Beloved One, Jesus He has for us."* Ephesians 1:5 TPT

THE VULNERABILITY OF LOVE

"We love Him because He first loved us." 1 John 4:19 NKJV

I realized as I studied the scriptures, that God had chosen to make Himself *vulnerable* to His love for me. To put it simply, He has given *all He is* to me through His Son Jesus, and that also means that I can actually hurt His heart. It is exactly the same way within the Covenant of my marriage to Anne-Marie. Her love for me has made her vulnerable to me, and I can actually hurt her through my choices.

Love in its purest form becomes completely vulnerable to the object of its affection!

As I kept discovering more of the Father's divine love for me, it gave my heart clear reason as to why I could not intentionally choose to hurt Him by living a compromised lifestyle as a believer. It was not from a 'rule' I keep, but a posture my heart takes to love Him only, as my Lord and my God! It's exactly the same way my love for Anne-Marie, stops me from intentionally hurting her heart.

By way of further explaining what I mean, let me create a 'today' scenario that will hopefully bring a graphic illustration of what my heart is trying to convey to you.

THE EX BOYFRIEND

Imagine my devastation as Anne-Marie's husband, if I picked up her phone one day and found a text from her ex-boyfriend - bad enough, but to see that she had also responded to him, and not just on one occasion, but frequently. No matter what she told me were the 'reasons' - my heart would be gutted, realizing a connection to her past had begun to stick it's ugly head into the sanctity of our marriage.

And to make matters worse, because I knew the full and tragic history behind her dysfunctional relationship with this man, I knew my hands were tied – she had made the choice to 'open the door' to his influence again, and my love could no longer protect her life. She was choosing to reposition her life and go outside the boundaries of safety that had been set up within our marriage. To make matters worse, I knew the full and tragic history behind her dysfunctional relationship with this man. I knew:

- He had not committed himself to the Covenant of Marriage with her...
- He had not given all he was to protect her for the rest of her life...
- He had not promised to love and cherish her above all others...
- He had not promised to care for her...
- He did not lay his life down for her...

Knowing the above to be true, my wife's ex boyfriend had *no* legal rights to her life now, however, her choice to 'open the door' invites the enemies of her past back into her life, sabotaging the future God had planned for her. The consequences are very real and very tragic.

This is also true for my life! I have made the decision that none of the 'ex' gods from my past life now can have any rights or access to my new life in Christ!

There is only One who I now give access to, and I choose not to 'text message' my past and go outside the boundaries of His Covenant love and safety for my life.

Marriage is the perfect 'picture' God uses to speak of His Covenant love for us as the Bride of Christ:

"And to the husbands, you are to demonstrate love for your wives with the same tender devotion that Christ demonstrated to us, his bride. For He died for us, sacrificing Himself to make us holy and pure, cleansing us through the showering of the pure water of the Word of God. All that He does in us is designed to make us a mature church for His pleasure, until we become the source of praise to Him – glorious and radiant, beautiful and holy, without fault or flaw." Ephesians 5:25-27 TPT

"Marriage is the beautiful design of the Almighty, a great and sacred mystery – meant to be a vivid example of Christ and His church." Ephesians 5:32 TPT

The greatest desire of the Father's heart, is that we become 'one' with Him and explore the unfathomable depths of His love for each one of us.

Paul's prayer in Ephesians says it this way...

"My dear friends I pray that...you will be empowered to discover what every holy one experiences – the great magnitude of the astonishing love of Christ in all its dimensions. How deeply intimate and far-reaching is His love! How enduring and inclusive it is! Endless love beyond measurement, beyond academic knowledge – this extravagant love pours into you until you are filled to overflowing with the fullness of God!" Ephesians 3:13,18,19 TPT

Our hearts were born for such a journey!

MY BEAUTIFUL BRIDE AND I ON OUR WEDDING DAY
3RD JANUARY, 2005

[YOGA ON TRIAL]

One of the most familiar New Age practices that is culturally acceptable, both inside and outside the church today is, of course, Yoga.

As I write this chapter, my heart is simply focused to bring a depth of understanding and wisdom to the reader regarding the practice of Yoga, both from my many years of training as a Master Practitioner of Hatha Yoga, and beyond that, through my latter years of intensive research into the origins of this Eastern practice.

As I present you with the factual history, including the origins and aims of Yoga, my hope is that this information will equip you to make a more informed and educated assessment of this practice and its role in your own life.

HOW THE WEST WAS WON

Hindu monks, beginning with *Swami Vivankananda* brought Yoga to the West in the late 19th century. He introduced Yoga to the World Religion Fair, Chicago, in 1893, saying:

"In America is the place, the people, the opportunity for everything new!"

Vivankananda had learned from his Guru, that the world's religions, *"Are but various phases of one eternal religion."* He also believed that 'spiritual essence' could be transmitted from one person to another. At the World Parliament of Religions in Chicago he began his discourse with these words, *"Sisters and brothers of America.!"* - the captivated audience immediately rose to their feet, giving him a standing ovation!

It was in this defining moment, that the 'love affair' between the West and East was born! This precipitated a continual stream of Eastern practices and philosophies flowing into the West.

In the 1920's and 30's, Hatha Yoga began to be strongly promoted in India with the work of *T.Krishnamacharya, Swami Sivananda* and other Yogis who practiced this form of Yoga. It is not an overstatement to call *Krishnamacharya* the 'father' of modern Yoga. He was an Indian Yogi and scholar, who claimed to have received his training in Hatha Yoga during seven years spent with his Guru, Ramamohana Brahmacharya, who lived in a cave in a remote region of the Himalayas.

Krishnamacharya also spent many years studying and teaching, not only philosophy, but Sanskrit, which is the primary liturgical language of Hinduism. He also mastered in Vedic rituals from the Vedic religion around 1500 BC. This became one of the major influences that shaped contemporary Hinduism.

In 1924 *Krishnamacharya* opened his first Hatha Yoga school in Mysore. There he discipled three students who were dedicated to the continuation of his legacy, including the increase and popularity of Hatha Yoga. One of his students, *Sivananda* was a prolific author, writing over 200 books on Yoga. He also established nine 'ashrams' - places of religious retreat, as well as numerous Yoga centers around the world.

In 1947 *Indra Devi*, her Russian name Eugenie Peterson, opened her Yoga studio in Hollywood. Up until this point, the importation of Yoga to the West still continued at a trickle, however, she was able to popularize Yoga in America through her many celebrity pupils in Hollywood. This earned her the nickname, *"The first lady of Yoga"*. Her biographer, Michelle Goldberg, wrote that Devi, *"Planted the seeds for the Yoga boom of the 1990's."*

In 1986 along with another 30 New Age Leaders worldwide, I was personally involved in a program to 'spearhead' the launch of Hindu practices into the West. This included Hatha Yoga. We were strategically 'armed' with a full arsenal of literature - all extolling the virtues of our New Age beliefs and practices. Like a well oiled machine, we travelled extensively, running back-to- back conferences and seminars throughout the year. We had literally thousands of participants world wide.

In 1992 an International Conference titled, "*The Dawn of a New Science*" was launched. It was designed to initiate a long range plan to have *Kundalini* and *Yoga* further embraced in the West. The more important 'push' of the Conference was to have Yoga's acceptance as a 'clinical entity' in Western society. *(taken from an article in "The Golden Age Magazine" issue 12, 1993)*

In 2013 Yoga is being practiced by some 20 million people in the US alone.

In 2016 Yoga is now being practiced by some 37 million people - an increase of almost double in just a few years.

In 2018 *The Yoga Journal* and *The Yoga Alliance* conducted a "*Yoga in America Study*", with the following results:

The top five reasons for starting Yoga were:

1. Flexibility (61 percent),
2. Stress relief (56 percent),
3. General fitness (49 percent),
4. Improve overall health (49 percent),
5. Physical fitness (44 percent).

It is interesting to note from the above survey statistics, that there was not one mention of the 'spiritual' ramifications for an individual practicing Yoga.

My knowledge as a Master Practitioner of Hatha Yoga qualifies me to tell you another story...

THE BIRTHPLACE OF HATHA YOGA

The most common Yoga practice in the West is Hatha Yoga. The word *Hatha* literally means 'force'. In the 20th century as Hatha Yoga, particularly the 'asanas', (which are the physical postures), became popular throughout the world, the name 'Hatha Yoga', became simply, 'Yoga'.

In India, Hatha Yoga is associated in popular tradition with the Yogis of the Natha Sampradaya through its mystical founder *Matsyendranath,* who is celebrated as a saint in both Buddhist and Hindu tantric and Hatha Yoga schools. (*tantric - the use of mantras, meditation, Yoga and rituals). Currently, the oldest dated text to describe Hatha Yoga, the *Amrtasiddhi* comes from a tantric Buddhist culture.

IGNORANCE IS NOT ALWAYS BLISS

The tendency in the West has been to dissociate Yoga from its source, which is an intimate part of the whole Hindu religious system. As a result, many practitioners see Yoga primarily as a technique for improving fitness and flexibility or reducing stress. Therefore, much of the emphasis of Western Yoga is on the perfection of the pose, stretching and exercise, which ultimately means that the *real and hidden meaning* of the actual religious practice behind Yoga, has been ignorantly left out.

This ignorance can be extremely dangerous, when Yoga is not recognized as an actual religious practice, but merely an exercise routine!

There is no denying Yoga exercises have clear physical benefits, however, the question we need to ask is:

"Can Yoga actually be separated from its religious ancestral roots?"

Throughout all my years of training in Hatha Yoga, I was taught that the physical and mental disciplines of Yoga were a powerful method to attain *'union with the divine'*. The *'divine'* being the spiritual realms and higher planes that exist beyond this natural realm. We were taught that Yoga techniques and disciplines were a means of reaching 'higher states of consciousness', with the promise that with enough practice, eventually we would reach the state of *enlightenment!*

During my training, I learned that Hatha Yoga is one of the six 'systems' of Hindu philosophy, and from which the modern practice of Yoga is derived. *The Yoga Sutras* is a complex, rigorous religious system involving multiple and varied 'asanas' or Yoga poses. This also includes breath-control, sense-withdrawal, inner contemplation, concentration, meditation and 'samadhi', or 'oneness' with the Hindu god, Brahman.

The actual meaning of the word Yoga is 'union'. It is derived from the Sanskrit root "yuj", meaning 'to join', 'to unite' or 'to subjugate'. It also means 'to control' and 'to discipline'. Our English word 'yoke' is also derived from the same Sanskrit (Indo-European) root.

THE TRUE GOAL OF YOGA

The ultimate goal of the practice of Yoga, is to 'yoke' or have 'union' with Hindu gods. This 'goal' is clearly identified through the study of ancient Hindu texts.

According to the religious texts of Hinduism and even Buddhism, you cannot separate Yoga from its spiritual aspects and outcomes.

In chapter 6 of the ancient Hindu text of the *Bagavita*, it reads:

> "There is joy as the pupil becomes one with Krishna",

Chapter 13 goes on to quote:

> "The real purpose of Yoga is to become yoked with the Hindu god Krishna and that he will live within you.
>
> Lord Krishna is the prince of demons."

The publication *Hinduism Today* has this to say:

> "Originating in India over 5,000 years ago Yoga was essentially handed down from generation to generation, from master to master.
>
> The simple immutable fact is that Yoga originated from the Vedic and Hindu culture. Its techniques were not adopted by Hinduism, but originated from it. The effort to separate Yoga from Hinduism must be challenged because it would run counter to the fundamental principles upon which Yoga itself is premised.

Efforts to separate Yoga from its spiritual center reveals ignorance."

Whether we are an advocate for Yoga or not, we must realize that *Yoga is rooted in spiritualism*, and many of the postures have a meaning that goes beyond simple strengthening and lengthening of muscles. This ancient form of exercise goes deeper into the connection between mind, body, and spirit, by using specific postures and poses, called 'asanas'.

Yoga is in no way as 'innocent' as a gym workout!

Ananda Marga Yoga Society – Jamalpur, Bihar, India (founded in 1955) by Prabhat Ranjan Sarker makes this comment:

"Physical Yoga, according to the classical definitions, is inheritably and functionally incapable of being separated from Eastern Metaphysics."

Along with the basic postures or 'asanas' in Yoga, breathing exercises called 'pranayama' are also practiced.

The ultimate purpose of *asanas* and *pranayama* is to purify the 'nadis' or nerve channels so that 'prana' can freely flow through them. Prana is described as being a 'vital energy' which must flow throughout the body, to prepare it for the raising of *Kundalini*, the supreme 'cosmic energy'. This 'energy' is released through 'charkas' (subtle psychic-energy centers) throughout the body, which activates the *Kundalini 'force'* that is lying dormant at the base of the spine. The 'energy/spirit' then travels up through the spine and the 'chakras', to ultimately be released from the head or crown chakra, to then have 'union' with the Hindu gods. The Yoga student has now entered into a state of 'god consciousness'.

The real and ultimate purpose of Yoga is to awaken the Kundalini spirit to move into your being and take possession of your body!

Kundalini, the 'vital energy' of 'prana' in Yoga is the 'spiritual entity' responsible for higher states of consciousness. However, this entity also brings a dark and sinister 'side effect' into the lives of those who ignorantly choose to awaken this energy force. *(I cover this in greater detail in the following chapter, The Gods of Yoga).*

During the last three decades, Yoga and meditation have gained greater popularity, as people have begun to express a desire for self-knowledge, and an understanding of higher states of consciousness. Unfortunately, many have embarked on their search without knowing the true aims of Yoga, nor with a full understanding of the 'spiritual entity' behind the promise of *higher states of consciousness!*

FURTHER WARNINGS

In my attempt to add more clarity to the Yoga question, I have chosen to highlight comments from a varied group of men and women who have gained high levels of mastery in the practice of Yoga. I believe their deep insights gained from years of experience in this Eastern practice, now qualifies them to give sound warning to others.

Article from *The Golden Age Magazine*, issue 12, 1993

"The activation of the energy in Yoga can be dangerous not only to the individual's sanity but also their life. The awakening of the energy can be accompanied by a complete physical and psychological upheaval. Unfortunately in the West, if this process is activated it can lead to enormous mental and physical suffering."

Excerpt from *The Inner Guide to Meditation* by Edwin Steinbrecher (1987)

"Emotionally the Kundalini may cause abrupt changes, the conditions are labelled 'anxiety attacks'. It can also cause psychotic episodes."

Swami Prabhavananda, an Indian monk of the Ramakrishna Order – moved to the USA in 1923 and founded the Vedanta Society of Southern California.

"Unless properly done there is a good chance of injuring the brain. Those that practice without proper supervision can suffer a disease which no known science or doctor can cure. Physical exercise of Yoga are designed to prepare the body for the spiritual change."

From the book *Yoga, Kundalini, An Occult Experience*, written by GS Arundle in 1938

(Arundle was 'pro' Yoga and part of a group bringing it from the East into the West)

"So many people are having these bad effects without even realizing it. The awakening of Kundalini is fraught with the utmost danger. It is related with the great occult rites of fire on earth. The universe, Kundalini which is the Lord un. It turns in a boomerang fashion with terrible effects upon those who misuse it. Upon those that do not reverence it. This serpent fire does not discriminate, it consumes.

Before anyone seeks to arouse the Kundalini let them know much about it. Especially its dangers."

Kundalini and the Secret of Yoga, Gopi Krishna – a Yogi

"It was variable for many years, painful. I passed through all the stages...for some time I was hovering between sanity and insanity. This book is about the account of what happens to the mind and body. It describes the perils, upheavals and other horrors about this force that is aroused in the practice of Yoga.

The real purpose of Yoga is to keep oneself always aware of Lord Krishna is within you."

The Tibetan Book of the Dead, Carl Jung, 1927

(Jung was also 'pro' Yoga)

> "One often hears and reads about the dangers of Yoga. The deliberately induced state which in certain unstable individuals might easily lead to real psychosis, is a danger that needs to be taken seriously indeed. These things really are dangerous and ought not to be meddled with in our typically Western way.
>
> It is meddling with fate, which strikes at the very roots of human existence and can let loose a flood of sufferings of which no sane person ever dreamed."

EXPERIENCE THAT DOESN'T LIE

With the above comments in mind, I want to flag something that I have been made aware of as a 'universal' result in the lives of those who practice Yoga as a lifestyle.

And that is...the fear factor!

In countless situations, I have come across those who struggle consistently with fear, anxiety, and/or experience frequent panic attacks, and even psychotic episodes - only to find out when I have 'dug deeper' that in 90% of cases, the individual is practicing Yoga!

The complete irony of this, is that the practice of Yoga is touted as 'the answer' that promises to bring relief to those experiencing such symptoms. However, the real truth is…

Yoga is the 'open door' that anxiety and fear walk through to take up legal residence in a person's life!

In our Western society today, fear, anxiety and psychosis are at an all time high – in fact, I believe, they have now risen to epidemic proportions in many spheres of our society!

THE TRUTH ABOUT FEAR

There are two great and powerful influences that motivate our lives.

One of them is fear…!

The Bible clearly teaches that fear is a "spirit" …*and one that does not originate from God's kingdom of light!*

"For God has not given us a spirit of fear, but of power and of love and of a sound mind." 1 Timothy 1:7 NKJV

We can also ascertain from this verse, that if, fear is a *"spirit",* and *not from God*, then it stands to reason that it's birth place is from the *realm of darkness*. As Yoga and Eastern practices are spawned from the same realm, it further stands to reason, that the *"spirit of fear"* can gain *legal access* to people's lives through their willing involvement with these practices. It's also interesting to note from the above verse that God talks about His 'will' being a *"sound mind"* - the very thing the enemy makes his target!

As a Minister of the Gospel, I am constantly being contacted by people who are beginning to ask themselves the 'hard' questions about Yoga. I am thinking of the young couple who are having problems in their marriage in areas of intimacy - the husband heavily involved in Yoga and displaying unhealthy and seductive approaches to other women. *(New Age spirits often manifest through seduction),* to the young Dad whose wife does Yoga, and has put her son into a Yoga class at school, only to be faced with their son having anxiety attacks and being advised, *"You need to medicate him"!*

The sad truth is... *you cannot medicate a "spirit of fear"!* You can offer medication to an individual to help alleviate the 'symptoms' of fear from their mind, their emotions and their physical body. However, these are all man's 'natural' remedies for an issue that is *spiritual* in its origin!

The above examples are but a tiny 'drop in the bucket' of people seeking answers to a subject that has been shrouded in mystery and ignorance in today's culture.

Thankfully...there is an answer!

THE TRUTH ABOUT LOVE

The second greatest influence that motivates the lives of mankind is love...!

The power of God's supernatural love through Jesus, offers each one of us complete and total freedom from every torment of fear.

"There is no fear in love; but perfect love casts out fear, because fear involves torment. But he who fears has not been made perfect in love." 1 John 4:18 NKJV

The enemy's mandate is to control our lives through fear. This includes fear in all its forms – fear of punishment, fear of rejection, fear of judgement, fear of failure, fear of criticism, fear of coronavirus, etc, etc. These 'fear motivators' can present themselves in endless and unhealthy 'life cycle' choices, as the soul of man attempts to rid itself of its constant 'voice' of torment!

Jesus boldly teaches us throughout His Word, that we don't have to live a lifestyle of 'maintenance', when it comes to fear related issues, but offers us *full and complete freedom* through the supernatural power of His love, and the authority of His Word.

"Let me be clear, the Anointed One has set us free – not partially, but completely and wonderfully free! We must always cherish this truth and stubbornly refuse to go back into the bondage of our past." Galatians 5:1 TPT

Over and over, I have witnessed Jesus bring people *full freedom and deliverance from the "spirit of fear"*, when they have chosen to renounce their New Age practices. I have also seen their bodies freed from illnesses that has afflicted them for years, and that the medical profession has been unable to find answers for. This has included people with excruciating back pain. I have seen them set free in one moment of encounter with God's healing love, and in many cases, I've heard the same words, *"I felt something travel up my spine and leave my body!"*

Does this sound familiar in in the light of what we've just learnt about the *"Kundalini spirit"* associated with Yoga?

"Your hand-to-hand combat is not with human beings, but with the highest principalities and authorities operating in rebellion under the heavenly realms. For they are a powerful class of demon-gods and evil spirits that hold this dark world in bondage." Ephesians 6:12 TPT

My evidenced conclusion is that Yoga is *not simply physical exercise* – it is spiritual in its origin and can carry dangerous consequences for those who practice it unknowingly.

In the following chapter I take a look at the most prevalent Hindu 'gods' behind the practice of Yoga, identifying their *true and dark personas!*

THIS WAS THE COVER OF A RECENT LIMITED EDITION
TIME MAGAZINE, MARCH 2020

Spiritual Evolution

15

[THE GODS OF YOGA]

Karel Werner states the following in his discourse from ***A Popular Dictionary of Hinduism*** (p.182) -

> *"According to the Hindu religious tradition it was revealed that even gods gained immortality and their supreme powers by the practice of Yoga."*

Theos Bernard makes this quote in ***Hindu Philosophy*** (p.86) –

> *"Remember the term Yoga comes from the root "yuj", "to yoke or join". It means the union of the individual spirit with the Universal Spirit."*

Since the greater majority of Yoga 'asanas' have Indian Sanskrit names, Yoga was a practice of postures dedicated to Hindu gods, with the supreme goal of achieving a *higher state of consciousness*, through a spiritual connection to those gods.

To further help you in your ability to make an informed decision as to the value of Yoga in your own life, I have given a brief description below, of some of the more 'common' Hindu gods that Yoga is dedicated to...

SHIVA

Shiva is the "destroyer of evil and the transformer" within the Trimurti - the Hindu 'trinity' that includes Brahma and Vishnu. *Shiva is commonly identified by the serpent around his neck. He also has a 'darker side' as the leader of evil spirits, ghosts and vampires.*

Shiva is also known as Adiyogi Shiva, regarded as the patron god of Yoga.

KALI

Kali was first introduced to the modern world by Ramakrishna Paramahansa as the Supreme Mother of the Universe. Through Ramakrishna - an avatar for many - the inspiration of Ma Kali awoke India to its ancient spiritual heritage and brought the unifying message of Yoga to the world.

Yoga in the true sense is a practice of 'mergence' and *return to the divine source of existence. Kali is the nirodha shakti, the 'power' of the Upanishads.* (Ancient Hindu Scriptures).

Kali is the 'inner power' of Yoga or Yoga Shakti.

Kali's earliest appearance is that of a 'destroyer'! *Kali* is the Hindu goddess (or Devi) of death, time, and doomsday. This goddess is often associated with sexuality and violence, but is also considered a strong mother-figure and symbolic of motherly-love. Over time, she has been worshipped by devotional movements and tantric sects variously, as the *Divine Mother and Mother of the Universe*.

Kali also embodies "*shakti* "- feminine energy, creativity and fertility - and is an incarnation of Parvati, 'wife' of the great Hindu god Shiva. *Kali* wears a garland of skulls and a skirt of dismembered arms. She holds a sword and a freshly severed head dripping with blood. She is the goddess of death, sex and violence.

Kali is often portrayed standing or dancing on her consort, the Hindu god Shiva, who lies calm and prostrate beneath her. Death and Destruction in Hinduism is not treated as the end, but a beginning.

Kali is still worshipped today by Hindus in many active temples throughout India.

KUNDALINI - LIFE FORCE

Kundalini energy is believed to reside in the realm of the 'great sleeping serpent' who is coiled along the base of the spine, and once awakened through devout meditation, slithers up the spine toward the pineal gland and through the crown 'chakra', ultimately moving one into *divine selfhood*.

This 'energy' represents the full potential of human awareness, and it's this coil of energy that is unleashed when the *Kundalini* is awakened.

This can happen in a number of ways, including the practice of doing 'asanas' or Yoga postures.

When the Kundalini is freed, it rushes up to the brain through a hollow tube in the spinal cord called the "sushumna". On its way to the brain, according to Swami Vivekananda in his book *Raja Yoga* -

> *"The energy unlocks layer after layer of the mind and the yogi is freed from the bondage of his ordinary earthly identity and achieves "samadhi" or complete union with the divine consciousness."*

The Yogi B.K.S. Iyengar Swami Vivekananda gives further warning in an excerpt from *Livestrong.com* -

> *"I liken the nervous system to an electrical system with wiring (the nerves), circuits (chakras) and gates or locks (bandhas). As with any electrical system, a power surge of Kundalini can damage the grid, causing grave mental and physical illness."*

Kundalini 'energy' is mentioned consistently throughout every discourse and spiritual 'diagnosis' on the aims and goals of Yoga.

In the following chapter I bring 'spiritual' context to the Yoga poses that we are most familiar with in our Western culture.

16

[THE ASANAS OF YOGA]

In Yoga, most of the postures or 'asanas' come from Hatha Yoga, however, not exclusively.

NE Sjoman makes the following observations in *The Yoga Tradition* -

> *Yoga is a spiritual body language from India. It was developed as a spiritual practice to unite with the Hindu divine and as a religious rite to worship the Hindu divine.*
>
> *Many of its poses and sequences of poses are inspired by Hindu mythology. Its active poses are devotion in motion, the embodied veneration of figures from sacred Hindu literature. **Active poses represent certain Hindu***

gods, creature beings, and sages after which the poses are named and patterned and to which they have been dedicated. The practice of such poses is a type of "role playing" of another spirit being, whether knowingly or unknowingly. The practice of such poses identifies a person with the Hindu Supreme. Yoga poses send messages to the spirit world, attracting spirits of Hinduism.

When you perform the body language of Yoga, spirits associated with Yoga respond to the call and the praise. Just as language has invocatory power, so too, body language has invocatory power. **Yoga is a full body "come here" signal; it is a full body "I adore" and "I implore" signal.** Those who are honored by poses named after them and dedicated to them and shaped after them show up to a performance in their honor. Of the 200 poses listed in Iyengar's Light on Yoga (1966), the landmark book that popularized yoga in the West, 33 poses are named after Hindu deities, children of deities, demigods, sages, and other mythological or legendary figures represented by the poses and invoking the qualities or spirits of those beings.

These poses might seem "neutral" to westerners, but they assume totemic significance in Yoga: shaping oneself into an animal or object in nature identifies the practitioner with that entity for the purpose of endowing the practitioner with the "spiritual power" and desired qualities associated with that entity.

Spirits do not require informed consent because they do not honor human will the way God does. They are glad that pagan worship inherent in Yoga is obscured as something beneficial and desirable: as exercise, a health and beauty regimen, and a performing art. But ignorance is never a defense, for spirits exploit ignorance; nor is unwillingness a defense if we participate; our participation sufficiently engages our will. We may say "No" to Hinduism in our minds, or "I'm not responsible for what I don't know," or "I could care less," but we say "Yes, I'm interested; yes, I'm invested" with our bodies. What we do is more important than what we think. **Doing Yoga constitutes informed consent.** The act of striking poses expresses willingness to receive all that Yoga is and gives spirits of Yoga a license to operate in our lives. **A practitioner who strikes a Hindu deity pose entertains the figure it represents and potentially courts any spirit attracted to it.**

Livestrong.com also states the following:

Hatha Yoga Pradipika lists 35 Yoga siddhas starting with Adi Natha (Hindu god Shiva) followed by Matsy-

endranath and Gorakshanath. It includes information about shatarma (6 acts of self purification), 15 asana (postures: seated, laying down and non-seated), pranayama (breathing) ad kumbhaka (breath retention), mudras (internalized energetic practices), meditation, chakras (centres of energy), kundalini, nadanusandhana (concentration on inner sound), and other topics. Yoga, in this context is one of the 6 āstika schools of Hinduism (those which accept the Vedas as the source of knowledge).

On the following pages, I have chosen to highlight 15 of the more common *asanas* that students of Western Yoga would be most familiar with:

NAMASTE

Greeting and Finishing Pose

What does Namaste mean?

The gesture Namaste represents the belief that there is a 'divine spark' within each of us that is located in the 'heart chakra'. The gesture is an acknowledgment of the soul in one, by the soul in another.

"Nama" means bow, *"as"* means I, and *"te"* means you. Therefore, *Namaste* literally means *"bow me you"* or *"I bow to you."* In Hinduism, it has spiritual import reflecting the belief, *"the divine and self (atman, soul), is the same in you and me"*, and connotes *"I bow to the divine in you."* In the ancient Hindu scriptures such as Tait-

tiriya Upanishad, as *"Atithi Devobhaa"* (literaly means, *"may the guest be god"*).

The placement of the hands has a very profound meaning within *Namaste*. The hands are full of nerve endings and it is believed the flow of Prana through the Nadis in the hands, can be as expressive, if not more, than the human voice. When the hands are placed together in the gesture of *Namaste (or anjalimudra)*, all the energies are levelled evenly as the hands are placed over *Anahata chakra* or the heart centre. (Wikepedia)

THE FISH GOD POSE

Ardha Matsyendrasana Asana with Namaste

Sanskrit name is *Ardha Matsyendrasana* which means half lord of the fishes.

THE DOWNWARD-FACING DOG POSE

Adho Mukha Svanasana

Deservedly one of Yoga's most widely recognized poses.

The name comes from the Sanskrit *"adhas"*, meaning 'down', *"mukha"*, meaning 'face', *"svana"*, meaning 'dog', and *"asana"*, meaning 'pose'.

The spiritual implication behind the pose lies in the act of a combined stretch with a moment in which *the yogi turns inward*, simultaneously connecting to his or her *center*, while stretching the body into a long line. This has a unifying effect *positioning the spirit within*, while you stay connected to the outside world.

Traditionally, this asana is believed to activate a number of the *chakras*, including the *manipura* and *ajna chakras*.

NB: Activating the manipura chakra through adho mukha svanasana is positioning yourself to come under the influence of spiritual entities that draw their "power source" from the kingdom of darkness.

THE SUN SALUTATION

The Sun Salutation is often one of the first series of poses done directly after seated breathing exercises, during morning Yoga sessions. The salutation is meant to *greet the sun* and is used as a way to *worship the Hindu sun god, Surya*, who is the symbol of health and immortal life. The 12 distinct poses of the Sun Salutation each have their own 'mantra' and the full series is directed towards *the celebration of the sun and the sun-god, Surya*

While performing the *Sun Salutation*, Yoga devotees are encouraged to think of the *flow of the pose*. They are taught the pose builds 'heat' and 'purifies the system' as the individual seeks *enlightenment, for what is higher consciousness*, while allowing themselves to be filled with 'light'.

THE COBRA POSE

Bhujangasana

It is along the lines of the spine that the 'inner' *Cobra* is channeled and stimulates the *swadhisthana* and *manipura chakras*. Just like the mystical snake charmers who were thought to have strong ties to the gods due to their 'magical' ways with cobras, Yoga devotees can tap into the divine space that resides along the lines of the spine through the power of the *Bhujangasana - The Royal Serpent!*

THE WARRIOR POSE

Virabhadrasana

Warrior Pose - there are three main poses and three other variations. They are all derived from the ancient story of a warrior named *Virabhadra, the son of Hindu god Shiva. (Shiva is the god of death and torment.)*

This pose is meant to 'channel' strength from the *Hindu god, Shiva* and *invoke the spirit of the great warrior* from whom this pose is named.

THE TREE POSE

Vriksasana

This pose has probably existed since at least the 4th to 5th century, BCE. Legends about Buddha and old texts called *Vedas (c. 1200 BC)*, describe *tapasic* which is *psychic heat-building practices* which included the Tree Pose.

In terms of Hatha Yoga and Kundalini science (*Kundalini Vidya*), the Tree Pose facilitates *ucchara*, which is the stimulation of *udana vayu* — the metabolic tendencies that *drive life' energy' upward in the body*. When the pose is held, the *'prana' (life force)*, goes *upward in the body*, and this is easy to feel through the balance of the Tree Pose. Upward-moving 'prana' facilitates the release of a more *transformative energy* called *Kundalini*, which also *moves upward from its source at the base of the spine.*

(The Kundalini and its destructive power was discussed earlier in this chapter)

THE CORPSE POSE

Savasana

The Corpse Pose, is usually the last pose in a Yoga class. It's a relaxation pose, performed while lying on your back on a mat. This pose is meant to *mimic death to help you prepare for it*. It's important to remember that the *yogic version of death* is different from the view held in the West. To the Hindu, death is seen as the *highest moment of life*, which is why this asana is an important Yoga pose.

THE HEADSTAND POSES

Salamba Sirsasana

Headstand Poses are among the most difficult for Yoga devotees to achieve, but they are also some of the most spiritually impacting poses.

Kundalini uses Headstand Poses to awaken and uncoil the "serpent energy" in the base of the spine bringing it to the crown of the head.

THE CAT /COW POSE

Marjaryasana/Bitilasana

The *Cat/Cow Pose* activates the *Swadhisthana chakra* - the second chakra. This pose is popular to practice as the cow is sacred to the Hindus and given divine standing as a 'god'.

This Yoga pose yokes you to the Hindu cow god.

THE PIGEON POSE

Kapotasana

Although people tend to think of *Kapotasana* as merely a bird-shaped asana, it is actually named after the *Master, Kapota*, whose yogic accomplishments are documented in Hindu scriptures such as the *Mahabharata* and the *Kalika Purana Garuda* -the mighty bird serving as a vehicle for the Hindu Lord Vishnu - one of the gods of the Hindu 'trinity'.

Yoga devotees are encouraged that if practiced properly, *Kapotasana* can take them to the *same level of accomplishment as the sage Kapota*.

THE EAGLE POSE

Garudasana

Garudasana is the name given to a 'divine creature'. A *garuda* is a huge, mythical bird with the golden body of a man, a white face, red wings, and an eagle's beak. He is supposedly the *king of the bird community*. Garuda is the vehicle of Lord Vishnu and the aspect of divinity which sustains the universe and takes birth as a man.

THE MOON POSE

Ardha Chandrasana

The moon is often associated with feminine energy.

The sun and moon are of central importance in Hatha Yoga - its name being derived from the *sun god ("Ha")* and *moon god ("Tha")*. Yoga offers to 'harmonize' opposing energies in the body attempting to balance the *'Ying Yang'* of darkness and light within.

THE BOW POSE

Dhanurasana This asana is the eighth pose in the 12 basic postures of Hatha Yoga. It is also the last of the three back-bending poses in a standard Hatha Yoga class.

As a spiritual practice, *Dhanurasana* stimulates the *manipura (solar plexus) chakra,* also called *'the life source chakra',* situated just above the navel. Stimulating this *chakra* increases *digestive fire* and *activates the flow of prana, or life energy (again, the origin of this energy source is inherently evil).*

THE WHEEL POSE

Chakrasana

The ancient texts of *tantra* and *Kundalini Yoga* hold this asana in the highest regard. In the *tantric tradition of Sri Vidya, chakrasana,* is used for *shakti chalana - the awakening of kundalini shakti,* the primordial 'pool of energy' and intelligence that resides in the human body.

NB: We know from our studies, that if an individual chooses to awaken the Kundalini energy force, they risk life changing consequences from the influence of a dangerous and evil spiritual entity.

Many Yoga devotees that I have spoken with over the years have defended Yoga by saying, *"I only do it for stretch exercises...!"*

As we have seen from the last 2 chapters, Yoga is much more than a 'stretch class' and can, in no way, be separated from the darker spiritual roots of Hinduism and its gods.

Below is a series of harmless stretches -

17

[THE WAY HOME]

Spiritual Evolution is a journey into the heart of God - a journey of discovery into the unfathomable grace and love of a good and kind Father…who I can now call my own.

This has been my story.

"But I know the way home, And I know that You will welcome me into Your house, For I am covered by Your covenant of mercy and love." Psalm 5:7 TPT

As you have journeyed with my heart through the pages of this book, my greatest desire is that you will have more answers for your life at the end of the book, than when you first began.

I have called this last chapter, *"The Way Home"*, simply because in my own life, I finally found that *truth* was, in fact, the *"way home"!* It was what my lost and wandering heart had always ached for.

It is the truth that...

- there is *only one God* that has loved mankind so intentionally that He sacrificed His own Son to pay the price for my sins.
- there is *only one God* that has freely welcomed me into an intimate relationship with Himself as his son.
- there is *only one God* whose heart longs to be near me as His child - to lead me, to guide me, to protect me, to counsel me and to bless me.
- there is *only one God* who has given the fullness of His inheritance to me through His Son, Jesus Christ - total healing for my body, soul and spirit - victory, peace, joy, provision, hope, and a brand new future and destiny.

"And there is salvation in and through no one else, for there is no other name under heaven given among men by and in which we must be saved." Acts 4:12 AMPC

I no longer need to risk punishment from the unseen enemy of my soul, nor be driven to 'perform' for the empty approval of man or a cruel religious system, based on lies.

"Before we knew God as our Father and we became His children, we were unwitting servants to the powers that be, which are nothing

compared to God. But now that we truly know Him and understand how deeply we're loved by Him, why would we, even for a moment, consider turning back to those weak and feeble principles of religion, as though we were still subject to them? Why would we want to go backwards into the bondage of religion...?" Galatians 4:8-10 TPT

SIMPLY BELIEVE

This is my God and perfect Father, who requires nothing more from me, other than I *simply believe* in His Son Jesus Christ and accept Him as my Lord and Savior.

"But Jesus loudly declared, The one who believes in Me does not only believe in and trust in and rely on Me, but in believing in Me he believes in Him who sent Me. And whoever sees Me sees Him who sent Me. I have come as a light into the world, so that whoever believes in Me may not continue to live in darkness." John 12:44-46 AMPC

"Because if you acknowledge and confess with your lips that Jesus is Lord and in your heart believe that God raised Him from the dead, you will be saved." Romans 10:9 AMPC

THE GIFT OF REPENTANCE

The "way home" is also the way of repentance!

For me repentance is a true 'gift' from God. It is where I admit that I have been wrong, and I make the choice to turn my life away from whatever I know has hurt the heart of God, and in that moment, I once again experience the true freedom that His forgiveness brings and the deepest assurance of His love for me.

"But if we freely admit our sins when His light uncovers them, He will be faithful to forgive us every time. God is just to forgive us our sins because of Christ, and He will continue to cleanse us from all unrighteousness." 1 John 1:9 TPT

AN ORPHAN BECOMES A SON

I heard a minister say once, that when a study was done on children who were orphans, they all shared one common factor... none of them had any dreams. They had no 'identity' and therefore they had no dreams for their lives.

In the same way that an earthly father gives his children identity, so our Heavenly Father tells us who we are. It's through our relational journey of love with Him, that we truly discover who we are.

"It's in Christ that we find out who we are and what we are living for. Long before we first heard of Christ and got our hopes up, He had His eye on us, had designs on us for glorious living, part of the overall purpose He is working out in everything and everyone." Ephesians 1:11-12 msg

My prayer for you at the end of this book, is that your heart can now come to the same conclusions as mine has...as He calls you 'home'...!

"Then you will be empowered to discover what every holy one experiences – the great magnitude of the astonishing love of Christ in all its dimensions. How deeply intimate and far-reaching is His love! How enduring and inclusive it is! Endless love beyond measurement that transcends our understanding – this extravagant love pours into you until you are filled to overflowing with the fullness of God! Never doubt God's mighty power to work in you and accomplish all this. He will achieve infinitely more than your greatest request, your most unbelievable dream, and exceed your wildest imagination! He will outdo them all..." Ephesians 3:18-20 TPT

God bless you with the truth...

Alan

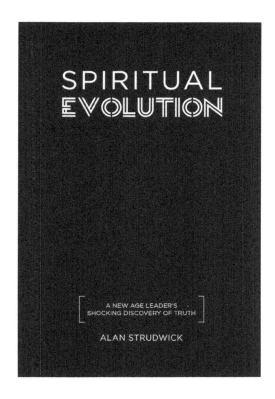

FOR ANY COMMENTS, QUESTIONS OR TESTIMONIES

PLEASE GO TO OUR FACEBOOK PAGE

@SpiritualEvolutionBook

[ALAN STRUDWICK MINISTRIES]

RESOURCES

www.alanstrudwickministries.com

www.kingdombusinessministries.com

Plus you can go to his YouTube Channel and subscribe in order to get FREE Resources

TO BOOK ALAN

contact@alanstrudwickministries.com

TO CONTACT ALAN

alan@alanstrudwickministries.com

If you have any questions, comments or need prayer please feel free to contact Alan direct on his email above.

Made in the USA
Monee, IL
11 November 2020